REVOLT AGAINST THE MADNESS

THE MADNESS

A PHILOSOPHY OF EROS OVER LOGOS

Salvatore Folisi

Also by Salvatore Folisi:

Walking The Streets in The Labyrinth of My Mind
(Originally published as *Daimon: A Journey of Poems*)

For Love of a Dark Night

Carnival of the Wild

Cover design by Rick Holland at Vision Press: http://myvisionpress.com/

ISBN: 978-1511739122

Published by Xander Stone Ink.
Second Edition/Second Publishing.

REVOLT AGAINST THE MADNESS

A PHILOSOPHY OF EROS OVER LOGOS

Salvatore Folisi

Previously Published Portions of
Revolt Against the Madness

★ A portion of "Giving Back to The Earth: A Reciprocal Way of Being in a One Way World" as "All Rationalist Doctrines Necessarily End in Nihilism" in *Adbusters Magazine* June, 2009.

★ "Human *Being* or Human *Going*?" in the online magazine *Reality Sandwich* (the brainchild of Daniel Pinchbeck) October, 2009.

★ "I Was Spared" in *Vision Magazine* June, 2010.

★ "Culture of Lost Souls in Search of a Profit" in the online journal *State of Nature,* Summer 2009.

★ "Human Beings, Technology & the Fate of the Earth" in *State of Nature,* Autumn 2009.

★ "Violence as Entertainment" in *State of Nature* Winter, 2012.

★ "Human *Being* or Human *Going*?" as "How Our Machine-based Way of Life is Not Only Destroying Nature, It is Destroying Us" on *AlterNet*, 2013.

★ "Strangers in a Strange Land" as "Why Are We All Ignoring Our Loneliness" on *AlterNet*, 2013.

★ "Violence as Entertainment" as "Is Violence in the Media a Reflection of Our Own Social Anxieties?" on *AlterNet*, 2013.

★ "Walking the Car or Driving Your Body?" in *Carbusters* (a Journal of the Carfree Movement), 2013.

Mitakuye Oyasin
For all my relations.

"Perhaps we have mistaken the path; perhaps the way out is to return to our origins."
~Octavio Paz, *The Philanthropic Ogre*

"The hard-hearted commercial cupidity, myopic dynastic political and religious stupidity, and the Earth- and people-hating spiritual amnesia sold to us as a forward-moving vision, by which we find ourselves barraged today, are nothing new at all, but a timeless, never-ending disregard for the female principle of life which has been with us for a long, long while, an anathema that needs to be composted into something out of which we can finally grow real cultures of grief, beauty, and peace."
~Martin Prechtel, *Long Life Honey in the Heart*

"Among the so-called neurotics of our day there are a good many who in other ages would not have been neurotic—that is, divided against themselves. If they had lived in a period and a milieu in which man was still linked by myth with the world of the ancestors, and thus with nature truly experienced and not merely seen from the outside, they would have been spared this division with themselves. I am speaking of those who cannot tolerate the loss of myth and who can neither find a way to a merely exterior world, to the world as seen by science, nor rest satisfied with an intellectual juggling with words, which has nothing whatsoever to do with wisdom."

~C. G. Jung, *Memories, Dreams, Reflections*

CONTENTS

Acknowledgements

I'd like to thank my family: my mother Joanne Fiske and her husband Pete Fiske for supporting me with a marvelous compassion throughout the writing of this book; my father Frank Falise for his lifelong support and encouragement of all my creative endeavors; and my late grandmother Margaret Broome who appreciated my philosophic ramblings since my teenage years and once told me she thought I could be a professor.

I'd like to thank *Adbusters* Magazine, *Vision* Magazine, *Reality Sandwich*, *AlterNet* and *State of Nature* for publishing early versions of portions of this book.

In some way, I feel myself to be part of a lineage of thought, a small link in an ongoing stream of inquiry about the meaning of human existence. As such, I wish to thank a collection of writers who have all made a profound impact on my own thinking— many of whom lived in previous epochs and have passed on to the other side of the mystery: Frederich Nietzsche, Jack Kerouac, Herman Hesse, Carlos Casteneda, John Lennon, Arthur Rimbaud, Carl Jung, Henry Thoreau, Alan Watts, Pablo Neruda, Sharon Olds, Robert Bly, James Hillman, Michael Ventura, Malidoma Somé, Octavio Paz, and Martin Prechtel.

I consider myself fortunate to have had some of the most remarkable teachers: Ron Oaks, Luigi Mulieri, Bonnie Morrissey, Jeffrey Allen, Shamms Mortier, Tom Verner, Dave Gershin, Phil Smith, Dennis Mead-Shikaly, and Garet Bedrosian.

Lastly, my friends who gave positive feedback as I wrote this book have made it all worthwhile: Chris Hale, David McLean, Jonah Salzman, Susan Kim, Greg Kemper, Jessica Hull, Kevin Lehrman, Gina Tang, Anna Horvitz, and Harry Polkinhorn.

The Philosophy of Eros Over Logos

The phrase "Eros Over Logos" came to me at some point during the writing of the book, signifying an imagined reversal of the prevailing philosophies and power structures in our society. At current, the paradigms by which we live are ordered by an over-reliance on logic and governed by an excess of reason that has reached its end in the irrational. They also impose suspicion on our instincts which debilitates our capacity for a direct and conceptually uncluttered experience of the world. As a society, we emphasize a limited and repetitive collection of traditional masculine qualities over the oceanic possibilities insinuated by an open-ended consideration of both the masculine and the feminine. Our national emblematic symbol, the eagle, flies high in the sky with the sun, pulling our attention away from the earth, away from the body, and away from the water of our emotions into an Apollonian realm.

This scenario describes the powerful rule we attribute to Logos as an ever-ascending complex of unilateral, though disembodied, *spiritual* and mental strivings, over Eros, which exists in the depths of our souls as the mysterious and dynamic underlying interplay of instinctual experience, bodily awareness, sensations, needs, feelings, imaginal impulses, archetypal callings and physical experiences in relationship to other bodies, the earth, and cosmos.

I wrote the essays in this book as a response, a rebuttal, a rebuking, and a revolt to the current social predicament in which we exist.

In modern society, Logos—as the *superior* and conceptual domain of the spirit and the mind—controls, manipulates, contorts, eclipses, and continuously strangles Eros—the *inferior* and experiential domain of the body and the soul. We empower Logos to accomplish this through multiple socially enforced paradigms, structures, and institutions. Thus, Logos provides the rules and restrictions, the taboos, the "do's and do not's," the sanctioned goals and ideals, and the mental constructs that frame, limit, minimize, and invalidate Eros.

Logos is equated with "the light"—as manifested by the Christian image of Heaven somewhere high up in the clouds—while all sorts of dangerous, dark bodily perversions and natural, earthly evils tend to be attributed to Eros. And yet, Eros dwells at the core of our being and without it we would be a living shell of a complete reality.

In Greek mythology, Eros was considered one of the first of the primordial gods who brought existence and all subsequent life into being. According to Hesiod, Eros (love) was the fourth of these gods to come into existence, following Khaos (air), Gaia (earth), and Tartaros (the underworld). In his *Theogony*, Hesiod proclaims Eros to be "the fairest among the deathless gods, who unnerves the limbs and overcomes the mind and wise counsels of all gods and all men." Thus, from the beginning, Eros provided a simultaneously destabilizing and transcending effect upon both gods and men. Like love itself, Eros is a bipolar force, pulling us into new life through the dark doors of death, or vice versa.

According to later accounts in Greek mythology, Eros is considered to be the son of Aphrodite and fell in love with, then courted, Psyche. This triage of forces presents quite a potent web of relationships. Of course, Aphrodite is well-known for her overwhelming beauty and has made her way into our modern lexicon through terms like "aphrodisiac," meaning a substance that arouses sexual desire. On the other hand, Psyche, in ancient Greece, referred to the soul and was symbolized by the figure of the butterfly, also a beautiful and mesmerizing creature. This image of Psyche is both earthly and ethereal, and indicates something telling about our deeper psychological natures.

Eros himself has also found his way into our modern verbiage as pertaining to erotic love. Although this interpretation is valid on its own ground, strictly speaking, it is not the meaning by which I understand the concept of Eros. My interpretation is more akin to the ancient cosmogonic understanding. Through this lens, Eros is indicative of immense, embodied psycho-spiritual and archetypal forces that are inclusive of sexuality, yet by no means exclusively sexual.

Robert Moore and Douglas Gillette have put forth a theory that Eros has two aspects: one being sensual and/or sexual—of the body—and the other being spiritual:

> The one drives the psyche "downward" to its archaic roots, and values the instincts from which human consciousness and human being arise. The other drives the psyche "upward" into realms that transcend individual Ego-consciousness, and perhaps even the biological foundations of the organism.

This is an interesting conception pointing towards the holism, or healing function, entailed in Eros. In this view, Eros is a dynamic and unifying force and can manifest in the *hot reds* of the body or the *cool blues* of the spirit, depending on the vessel or instrument or being through which it flows.

Eros is also a numinous and primordial energy in connection with Gaia, or the earth, as evidenced and expressed through the resplendence, the sumptuousness, and the gorgeousness of all creation. In line with this perspective, Carl Jung claimed:

> Eros is a superhuman power which, like nature herself, allows itself to be conquered and exploited as though it were impotent. But triumph over nature is dearly paid for. Nature requires no explanations of principle, but asks only for tolerance and wise measure.

The reality of Eros denotes the recognition that the body and the earth are the foundational *prima materia* of existence. The human mind and technological society have arisen out of the body and the earth, but—contrary to our unconscious assumptions—cannot function independently of them. Areas of endeavor such as environmental protection and climate change have evidenced the human impact on the earth. In line with Eros, my area of inquiry is more over concerned with the impact of a technology-centered society on the experience of the human soul, as manifested by an ill-aligned relationship between our consciousness, our bodies, and the earth. As a point of reference, I also strive to contrast our modern society with earth-centered cultures in which the human soul is celebrated through a continuous practical and ritual realignment of body and earth with human consciousness.

To a large degree, we have lost touch with the true primacy of the almost symbiotic relationship between the earth and our bodies. I don't know that the earth truly needs us, but I believe we have the capacity to manifest an evolved consciousness of the spiritual reality of the planet. As such, the earth and the body are not merely biological constructions of matter; they are highly intelligent physical containers/embodiments/carriers of the life force. This life force is the principle of the divine or sacred basis of existence. This life force breeds wonder, impels fascination, and moves through all living beings on this living planet magnificently in a complex, dynamic continuum, of which we humans are only one part, one portion, one aspect.

There is probably no greater teacher than the earth. Yet we often times fail to see this because we have built up our techno-industrial societies all around us—blocking our interface with nature and coagulating the inherent flow of energy, of life force, back and forth between the body and the earth. Yet we need this life force, this flow of life, this energy, experience, and inspiration. A rootless tree dies. And when we are cut off from our connection with our origins, with the earth, we as people get sick and part of us dies too.

This book is a collection of messages that envisions Eros in a more balanced and harmonious relationship with Logos in our society and throughout the human race. Ultimately, it hopes to point beyond the sad condition of our current state of imbalance and disharmony, to the possibility of living in connection with the planet, of acknowledging the profound reality of earth and body, and rejoining our souls and spirits with Life.

INTRODUCTION

Revolt Against the Madness was written from late 2008 through early 2009. I left it alone for a year or so, then gradually began the slow and intermittent work of editing the original notebook ramblings into something "presentable to the public." On the whole, it is comprised of a collection of rampant essays that explore how human beings and society have changed radically over the very recent period of our modern technological developments—and how these changes affect not only the earth itself, but our relationship to the earth, to ourselves, and to one another. The essays postulate that through our proliferation of an ever-increasingly technological way of life, we have left something of our original nature behind, something of *who* and *what* we are—which has now receded to a silent recess of our secret recognition.

Our self-forgetting and forgetting of the earth are coincident; through forgetting where we came from—the planetary origins of our evolution—we have also forgotten the ancient and most meaningful portions of ourselves, our true soul nature that can only exist in the context of the earth environment from which we have emerged.

The knowledge we have forgotten is not a collection of cerebral equations, nor can it be replaced by scientific inquiry or solutions; rather, the knowledge we have forgotten is cellular, experienced in our bodies and our consciousness through an ongoing, direct, and experiential relationship with a living and interactive planet.

True knowledge is not formed from the neck up. It begins in the soles of our feet and moves up through the entire body, bone by bone, organ by organ, circulating through the veins, the heart, the brain, the mind, and the spirit. True knowledge does not transcend or exclude the body; it is experienced through the body.

However, true knowledge and meaningful experience are not the primary goals of modern industrial and technological societies. To the contrary, our current mode of society aims towards more abstract goals and ideals, envisioning a *mechanically perfected* human species liberated from all the old burdens of struggle and strife with an unruly planetary environment.

More than extrication from an embedded, embodied engagement with the physical-spiritual matrix of the earth, our fragmenting social agendas advocate new laws, regulations, and restrictions every day that further impinge upon our personal freedoms and forbid us from enjoying our messy human condition. With the *progress of society*, ideas of wrong and right become more stringent and constricting, while our innate bodily pleasures become trampled by technological demands and the myopic moralizing of the mainstream.

As a creatively critical voice of social commentary upon how we are supposedly progressing as a human species and society, the perspective of social critique asserts that if we forge ahead blindly, simply accepting and adopting every new technological development and social trend presented, we become in danger of acting without full focus, without a well-rounded vision of our social, psychological, and environmental situations and their practical implications upon how we live, think, feel, communicate, and experience ourselves and the world.

Reflecting upon our way of life is an essential part of living. When we look at our world we should see something of ourselves in it, a place for who we are alongside evidence that who we are has been taken into consideration in the creation of such a world. If we do not, we are in danger of becoming devoured by something foreign to ourselves and losing our sense of self, as well as, perhaps, portions of that deeper mystery we call our soul.

The impetus to write this book stemmed from experiences of discontinuity between myself and the world. Although much of the book may be viewed as a form of complaint, writing it entailed a necessary and creative process for me to establish a greater sense of self in a world that often times and in many ways falls short of reflecting, nurturing, or encouraging who I perceive myself to be and what I imagine we as a human community are capable of becoming.

❖

AN UNDERLYING THEME of *Revolt Against the Madness* proposes that our ecology and psychology are two sides of an interrelated unity; hence, crisis or health in one region will profoundly affect the other. This realization instigates the question: how does the increasing gap between humans and nature over the course of our technological advancements influence our empirical, or experiential, sense of reality? From what I see, we are often times at odds and alienated in a machine-based world.

In this modern era, our chief concern as a global humanity is that of re-evaluating and integrating our industry, technology, and capitalism into functional forms that support the recovery and well-being of both our psychology and ecology. Throughout the book, this endeavor is also explored as part and parcel of respecting the continued existence of non-modern, *non-Westernized* cultures—and the belief systems they represent—who rely upon a holistic way of life within the natural environment which is now so vulnerable to the onslaught of modern technological society.

I realize there is no perfect society, no purely ideal way of life. However, it is of vital importance to examine the mistakes we've made and continue to make, and to contemplate the consequences of many social changes which have been virtually instituted into our human society and our psyches in a very short period of time as regards our overall evolution on the planet.

Our modern consumption of and by technological forms of capitalism contributes to controversial mutations of our bodies, minds, and spirits, our sense of and capacity for community, our relationship with the earth, and the rightful place of nature in our culture. Therefore, we must take into consideration not only how our new way of life is affecting ourselves, but how it is affecting the evolution of countless other species and life-forms in the biosphere.

In the final analysis, this book hopes to allure the reader's attention to a thoughtful reflection upon the interactions between the individual, society, and nature—and between the body, mind, and soul. As a creative self-world examination, or an expansion of consciousness into areas you might not normally consider, my hope is that something on these pages, even if it's only one essay or one sentence, awakens by means of resonance some meaningful awareness inside you.

Lastly, I owe much credit and inspiration for these writings to a handful of seminal thinkers who have cleared a path for me to walk: Octavio Paz, who embodied superbly the spirit of critique in his masterful work on the plight of Mexican culture, *The Labyrinth Of Solitude;* Michael Ventura, whose essays from *Letters At 3AM: Reports On Endarkenment* impelled me to think deeply about how social, personal, and archetypal realities meet, bend, and dance with each other—deceiving and illuminating one other simultaneously; John Trudell, whose fierce vision and honest voice speak out about the disparaging of the human heart in the modern world; and, Malidoma Somé, who, more so than any other teacher, has given me insight into the experience of the underlying soul upon which our fragile human lives and propensity for a planetary community float.

I

GIVING BACK TO THE EARTH:
A Reciprocal Way of Being
In a One Way World

THE MODERN WESTERN MIND operates mainly through the channels of rationality and reason. Because we seem to have attained a status of virtual mastery over our environment to acquire what we need or want, we have little interest in the more profound dimensions of that living environment, the limitless *beings* of nature, or our potential relationship with those beings and forces, that surround us—with whom we live and die, and upon whom we depend for our ongoing existence. However, regarding the whole of humanity over our entire span of evolution upon this planet, the modern Western perspective may in fact be the exception to the general rule, an anomaly, or at least merely one perspective among many that have served and in various ways enriched humanity down through the millennia.

Pre-Western modes of humanity—which have also been termed "native," "indigenous," and "primitive"—emphasize the faculties of intuition, sensation, and feeling more potently in their focus upon the interrelationship of human beings with the multifarious manifestations of the natural world. Pre-Western perspectives also employ these faculties in discerning spiritual forces at play through this world of created forms, of living creatures whose life-force according to these perspectives is both a mystery and a blessing, and whose origins can possibly only be imagined.

In his autobiography, *Lame Deer Seeker of Visions*, the author—a 20th Century Native American *yuwipi*, or shaman-healer—states, "The spirit is everywhere. Sometimes it shows itself through an animal, a bird or some trees and hills. Sometimes it speaks from the Badlands, a stone, or even from the water." In this paradigm of co-existence *within the web of life*, human beings take what they need with a certain measure of piety from the world of living creatures. They also have particular, even religious, ways in which they *give back to the earth*, and so to the spiritual presences or realities which are intuitively felt to have expressed themselves through the earth. Therein lies a profound difference which distinguishes the pre-Western from the modern Western mind-set.

According to Malidoma Somé, a medicine man from Burkina Faso, West Africa who leads international workshops on ritual, healing, and community—author of the book *Of Water and the Spirit*—in his indigenous African culture the first serving of a meal is given back ritually to the earth from which it came, as an offering of thanks for having been granted the food needed to sustain body and life. To the modern Western mind this may seem to be both wasteful and ridiculous because, rationally speaking, it makes no sense—we think of the homeless and the hungry, of people who are starving, and also remember how as children we were admonished to eat every scrap upon our plates. However, when viewed through an intuitive and symbolic lens, the act of serving the first dish to the earth is not only beautiful, it also conveys a feeling of connection and relationship with the greater mysteries and powers of the earth with whom we are in constant communion—if only through involuntary process such as the force of gravity, continual sensory intake of our surroundings, and every breath we take.

Giving back even the first bite of an entire meal to the earth is an act of humility and a way of at least attempting to strike a balance in our relationship with the awesomely generative and nurturing natural world. It is a way of communicating thankfulness and appreciation as well as acknowledging and in some small way honoring the incredible miracle of our lives upon this planet. Giving back to the earth is akin to, and complicit with, the prayer that precedes the devouring of the meal which is composed of an animal and/or plant that lost its life so that we could continue our own.

In the modern Western forms of Christian prayer we tend to think of, and thank, God for the meal; but pre-Western spiritual views tend to view *God the Creator* as implicitly synonymous with *God the Creation*. Asserting this view from a Native American perspective, Lame Deer states, "But all animals have power, because the Great Spirit dwells in all of them, even a tiny ant, a butterfly, a tree, a flower, a rock." In these modes of understanding, God is not merely hiding out or waiting for us far away in an undisclosed spiritual dimension, as a theoretical authority figure who has the power to grant us a final redemption or rejection at the conclusion of our earthly lives. In most earth-based religions—which are generally termed "animism"—the spirit of God is felt to inhabit the landscape and to live very close to humankind and to every other creature as well.

Although God may ultimately be considered to be a mystery, to the pre-Western way of thinking *God the Creator* is also evidenced, and so sensed and related to, through this physical realm of animals, plants, trees, rocks, rivers, earth, sun, planets and stars—not to mention human beings—as *God the Creation*. As Lame Deer so poignantly sums this up, "All of nature is in me, and a bit of myself is in all of nature." Therefore, to this sort of mind set, giving back an actual portion of the meal—a creative transformation of earth materials enacted by human beings through labors of love and preparation—would be viewed as a significant gift. What also seems significant about this ritual and the thinking that underlies it is its emphasis on *the importance of not just taking from the earth, but of also giving back,* thereby achieving some sort of balance through returning the *gift of life* to the *source of life*.

Even if the earth and the perceived spiritual forces moving through the earth have no literal need of ingesting food, the human act of *feeding the planet* denotes an attitude of respect, responsibility, care, and nurturing which perhaps has positive repercussions in humankind's ongoing needs for survival, as well as our needs for maintaining a set of ethics, morals, and philosophical principals that inform and guide our relationships with the earth and Her creatures.

Lamentably, through our current lifestyle we mainly excel at "giving back" gargantuan loads of trash to the earth: as excessive random litter and unending garbage into landfills; continual toxic wastes, oil spills, industrial runoff, and sewage into the rivers, lakes, and oceans; and tons of pollutants via cars, factories, refrigerators, and other forms of industry into the skies.

In essence, what modern civilization feeds the planet is mainly poison.

Not only that, we are taking more and more and more through our constant *development* of land, deforestation, and overall mining of the earth's natural resources. Although we tend to believe that we have evolved beyond the mentality and overall capacity of the pre-Western mind-set, there is obviously much we can learn from rudimentary reflections upon their perspectives and everyday practices. And though we triumph the victory of reason and rational thinking over the "foolish and outdated" ways of primitive cultures—with their superstitions, rituals and symbolic thinking—it is obvious that they still have some very important lessons to teach us.

In this current era, in which there is such monumental damage being done to the earth and biosphere through modern industry and technology, the practice of *giving back something nourishing to the earth* is a profoundly enlightening instruction on modifying and improving our relationship with the planet. Perhaps what must change first is the philosophy of living that underlies our interactions with all the other *beings* that also comprise the earth. When almost everything about our culture is infused with the feeling of domination over the earth, *we forget that in essence we are primarily earth creatures*, earth beings, human beings that cannot survive or thrive without a thoughtful and considerate way of life that takes the greater whole of earth, atmosphere, and universe into account.

We have insulated ourselves from the surrounding ecological environment in many ways. We tend to study, work, and play mainly in our own enclosed, human-made, indoor environments, wherein the only emissaries of nature may be a dog or a few plants. As a species, we've isolated ourselves from the panorama of our fellows such that we conceive of human life as something almost entirely separate from life as a whole on the planet—for, amongst all the species, only humans live the vast majority of our lives in boxes: from our homes, to our schools, to our offices, cars, shopping centers, malls, movie theatres, coffee shops, bars, restaurants, roller rinks, bowling alleys; even many of our newer sports stadiums are now enclosed "domes." This list of course does not account for our television, which is the box that most of us *live our lives through* on a daily basis.

What is this propensity we've developed for shutting the natural world out and enclosing ourselves inside our own self-created environments? Are we compensating for some secret fear of being devoured or destroyed by the very planet which we are steadfastly devouring and destroying ourselves? We of the modern Western world view ourselves as belonging to an exclusive club in which we, and only we, have inherited the right to claim whatever we want from whoever we want, without regard to the consequences of our actions on other (mainly non-Western and pre-Western) people, or on the other species and ecosystems of the earth. We have developed an entitled perspective in which we must have limitless access to limitless choices and options for satiating ourselves—and we must have what we want right now! But does this attitude not also belie an unconscious state of chronic dissatisfaction with our lives in general?

Through giving back something of intrinsic generative value to the earth, either literally or symbolically, in the form of food, prayer, sacrifice, or heartfelt offering, we receive the satisfaction and the encouragement that *we are of this world*, that we have enough to share a little and to acknowledge our co-existence with other creatures and planetary forces. Giving back doesn't have to be an elaborate or pretentious ritual that makes us feel awkward; it can simply be a small gesture or action that signifies one's compassionate interconnection with the world. We can be both creative and inventive in how we choose to give back to nature, to the planet, or the cosmos. What matters most is integrating this awareness into our daily lives so that an ebb and flow, a give and take, a mutually benefiting and reciprocal relationship can be consciously manifested.

Adopting a reciprocal way of being quite possibly invokes the kind of attitude and energy that is needed to help save humanity from extinguishing ourselves from the face of the earth. I offer these ideas as concepts which may be pondered and applied as one wishes, and in one's own unique way. Perhaps affirming and integrating a few ancient principals which have maintained harmony on the planet for millennia can help to guide us in a time when our own way of life is threatening to eradicate all sentient beings.

NOTE: In pre-Western paradigms, *the environment* is less harshly or distinctly delineated from *the person* or from humans as a species. In other words, in these modes of living, *human beings conceive of and experience themselves as being part of the environment,* as being inseparably related and identified with "the environment." The environment is, in essence, the part of you that exists outside the boundaries of your physical body. The environment is also, in essence, part of you, because without an "environment," there would be no "you." The environment becomes part of you through your senses, your mind, your body, thoughts, feelings, and behaviors. To every other human, and to every other living being, you are part of their environment, just as, to you, they are part of yours. Your environment defines and shapes who you are, just as you define and shape your environment. The modern world has more poignantly attempted the separation of the human being from their environment than any other culture, however impossible this may be.

II

HUMAN BEINGS, TECHNOLOGY
& THE FATE OF THE EARTH

I T'S BOTH FUNNY AND SAD that as soon as people leave
their familiar comfort zone, when they are alone, say at a coffee shop or waiting in line for a bus, they automatically, almost reactively, reach for the cell phone to call or text someone
who will reconnect them with the safe and familiar world from
which they have momentarily wandered away. The average person's lack of ability or willingness to encounter *an unknown situation* reveals a lack of tolerance for being alone, as well as a lack of
curiosity or propensity to simply notice and appreciate their surroundings—as though this were some dangerous proposal in
which their sense of self would quickly fragment should they let
go a little, observe, and potentially interact with the newly unfolding world around them.

Yes, we've learned to live in little bubbles of safety which cut
us off from our fellow humans. We no longer live fully in the actual world, but moreover in our own self-created realities via the
latest form of technology. I suspect that our modern sense of se-

curity has been entrained to operate in collusion with these technological devices that have slyly entrapped our minds even as they have offered us incredible new possibilities. Our reliance on new and ever-advancing technologies, such as the mobile phone—which in a few short years has also become a mobile photo album, mobile internet, camera, video machine and multi-media entertainment center—has developed into quite a habit, an unconscious addiction that is shaping the very nature of our personalities, and even, God forbid, our souls.

What need have we, the general public, for an imagination when so many limitlessly stimulating devices are available to us? Our inner worlds are increasingly programmed by the outer world of our own modern creations, by technological forces that have become so evocative, so seducing, so ever-demanding, evasive, and totalitarian that we simply obey the instructions they give us. We are continually inundated with advertisements and societal pressures to acquire new technological distractions and modes of external stimulus. Living under such conditions, how is it possible for us to maintain or cultivate much of an inner world of our own making, *or a soul*, whatsoever?

The underlying message of our media is commercial. In enforcing the demands of commerce upon us, we are defined primarily as consumers, persuaded not to think for ourselves, but to join in the latest collective frenzy of technological adventures that continually reinterpret the purpose of our lives. This never ending flood of media proclamations, while appearing as a material liberation, has become a psychological oppression and enslavement of the individual soul. Capitalism constantly sells new versions of reality that may have nothing to do with our true needs, desires, or sensibilities; however, it is the advertiser's job to convince us otherwise. So far they are doing a pretty good job!

The natural world—the land, the air, the trees, the vast realms of animals, plants, oceans, deserts, and mountains—is increasingly losing popularity and value in the self-hypnotized, narcissistic lives of mechanized human beings. Although it is certainly an abomination of our essential heritage, we are ever-entrained to focus less and less on the natural world, and more and more on the world as fashioned through the minds and hands of men.

It's sad indeed when we ignore the natural environment and, instead, remain culled to a collective techno-vision of the ideal man-made life. It's also sad when we ignore those human beings who are standing right in front of us because we'd prefer to text or talk with someone miles away—or chronically inhabit our digital handheld reality—because we've lost our human capacity for interrelationship with our expanded world of fellow citizens who we now dismiss as strangers.

Our advance in technology has engendered a compensating inversion in our capacity for compassion and community—which is to say, the further we develop our technology, the less we appear to maintain the qualities of a loving, caring, and attentive human society.

Being aware in the mystery of the present moment, tolerating the unknown, and tolerating states of non-stimulation or non-engagement with technological devices may be the first phase in moving towards a more attuned state of openness and potential interaction with the actual, non-virtual, world around us. However, we have been so conditioned by a perpetual bombardment of electronic stimuli—radio, television, computers, video games, mobile phones, iPods, and *iReality*—that it has become difficult, albeit unappealing, for us to refocus our attention on our natural, physical environment. Not only is it harder for us to engage physical reality over virtual reality, it is also increasingly difficult for us to engage natural reality over man-made reality. This is only augmented by the fact that we are increasingly surrounded by industrial and commercial environments that have replaced the original environments of nature.

A parallel outcome of our desensitization to the physical, natural world in which we live is the subsequent degradation of our ecology, which entails our lack of emphasis or awareness on its living-breathing-fragile-organic nature. The danger of this, as many of us recognize, is potentially catastrophic. As we create and live in an increasingly man-made and virtual reality—wherein we believe we are safer, happier, and more satisfied—we also increasingly ignore the actual and natural, immediate and physical reality in which we are encompassed and risk the extinction of the environment through the excessive polluting, raiding, and deforestation of the planet that we have witnessed since the rise of the industrial-technological age.

The degradation of the natural world is problematic in many ways. Firstly, it appears to be morally and ethically wrong—at least to those of us whose ethics and morals outweigh our capitalistic drives—to so harshly and destructively impact the earth and its ecosystems. One might ask, "What right have humans to destroy the earth simply for our own benefit? Is this not selfish and unnecessary?" Many of us have asked these questions, though it seems that the overall progress of our technologically-based capitalism remains unwilling to curtail its invasions and usurpations of nature or to halt its path of destruction for the sake of morals, ethics, or in the name of compassion for other living beings.

Why is this?

Because in capitalism, *where the dollar bill is concerned, questions of right and wrong become thin and ineffectual*, almost nearly meaningless. Survival and materialistic progress reign paramount.

Secondly, the degradation of the natural environment is increasingly affecting the balance of the planet itself, which in turn contaminates our own quality of life. For a thorough overview of how human technology is damaging the planet one has only to search through the plethora of books, TV specials, or movies on this topic. I will mention here only a few ways I have witnessed in which planetary degradation affects human life.

In a recent trip to Lima, Peru I learned that Peruvians predominantly drive older used cars, from the 70s or 80s, which emit high levels of toxic fumes. I suppose Peru does not yet have the infrastructure for emissions controls, and the people are typically materially indigent and probably couldn't afford it if such strictures were implemented. Therefore, the air is putrid with visible exhaust fumes. Driving around town there is often no escape from these fumes which pour out of the car just in front of you. I was both startled and shocked by this because it was nearly impossible to breath anything but very foul exhaust while driving.

The situation is just as bad in many other developing "third world" countries around the globe. Even here in the United States, where we have increasingly stricter emissions controls on our vehicles, the air quality in some cities is very poor, and on certain days people are advised to avoid going, or allowing their children to play, "outdoors" at all. In many countries, air pollution is severe and debilitating, and only getting worse. In addition to increasing the risk of respiratory disease, the profusion of pollution has led to eroding of the ozone layer, which has also increased the risk of skin cancer, such that it's become customary to slather on gobs of sunscreen lotion before going outside on a sunny day for any length of time.

Industrial pollution has also contaminated our public water supplies so they must be zapped with chlorine to be potable, making our water not really enjoyable or, many would agree, healthy to drink. Regarding our food, as genetic engineering takes hold, what we eat becomes increasingly tasteless and less nutritious. Although these are only a very few examples of the many problems made by technology, there is no denying that the degradation of the natural world leads to the degradation of our own human lives.

The third major impact of the degradation of nature is spiritual. As we become less attuned to the world of nature, which is gradually breaking down, our inherent connection to the earth dissipates. We become less the "caretakers of the earth," or participants in Her splendor of glory, and moreover the survivors of a man-made holocaust inflicted upon nature. We rationalize our disconnect from nature—those of us who are aware of it—with the heralding of a new age of technological transcendence. In comparison with all our own amazing discoveries, inventions, and developments we cannot believe that the earth is all that important. How can a handful of dirt or a muskrat compare to the glory of an iPhone?!?

OUR ACTIONS REVEAL an underlying belief that we are superior to the earth, evidenced by our collective science fiction fantasy to take off in rockets from the ground and be propelled into some new incredible cosmic techno-dimension. While this is an interesting fantasy—and probably more of a literalization of a spiritual or psychological process—it is not, in reality, very likely. Although I have heard there is scientific investigation into creating hospitable conditions on other planets, as well as expanded, city-size space stations in which we could begin to populate the greater universe and where we would, even more so, live in man-made, virtual reality realms.

The bigger question is whether our spirits can survive—or thrive—in states of stark disconnection from the earth, our origin and planetary source of being ...

This sort of fantastic and futuristic evolution is in line with our reigning religion of Christianity in which our sinful earthbound lives are to be potentially transformed through belief in Christ, whereupon the moment of our death we are to ascend high into the heavens, into a cloud-like dimension above and beyond all the messy entanglements of this planet earth. With such a cosmovision, such a context of the goal of life, it's no wonder the sanctity of the earth has lost its power to impel our actions. It seems only the portended threat of our own extinction will suffice to encourage us to behave differently.

Christianity also teaches that, of all the creatures and lifeforms upon this planet, only human beings have souls and can be "saved"—thus, only humans can make the transmigration beyond a mortal death into an immortal and eternal afterlife. Since, in the Christian view, nothing else upon this planet has a soul or is capable of redemption, we justify our own paramount importance, and it has become completely plausible to view all things as merely our own resources. In this way, we lose a perspective of value and veneration for the natural world around us while worshipping our own agendas.

It becomes evident that many areas of our lives—our economy, technology, industry, religion, and general philosophy of living—depict our own implicit superiority complex over the natural world of creation. And yet, by and by, we get glimpses of the truth that it is impossible for humanity to become superior to nature because we are intrinsically interconnected *with* nature: the earth, air, water, and sky which we seek to dominate and control. In actuality, nature is superior to humankind, as we are merely one aspect, one manifestation of its nearly infinite panorama. However, we continue to ignore our interconnectedness with nature and our true identity as the human expression *of* nature, and behave as if we have the ability to dominate the earth without eventually destroying ourselves. But, "what goes around comes around," and sooner or later you get what you give. Or to put it in technological terms: you "input" what you "output."

Why have we continued to develop our society in this succinctly shortsighted and unintelligent manner? I think the truth is that we really are out of control, so fascinated by our own invented civilization that we fail to recognize the greater organic and historical context in which we live. Over the past five hundred years or so, the peoples of Europe have invaded, conquered, colonized, and converted virtually every other continent, people, and culture upon the planet—we're currently working steadfast on the Middle East—with our imperialistic quests for a global democracy through Christianity and capitalism. Though we feign to admit it, money has become our new god.

Martin Prechtel, author of *Secrets of the Talking Jaguar* and an initiate of the Mayan shamanic mysteries, summarizes the spiritual and cultural devastation enacted through the rampages of imperialism which are truly essential to the foundations of modern industry, capitalism, and the establishment of Western democracy:

> Over the last two or three centuries, a heartless culture-crushing mentality has incremented its progress on the earth, devouring all peoples, nature, imagination, and spiritual knowledge. Like a big mechanized slug, it has left behind a flat, homogenized streak of civilization wherever it passed. Every human on this earth—African, Asian, European, Islanders, or from the Americas—has ancestors who at some point in their history had their stories, rituals, ingenuity, language, and lifeways taken away, enslaved, banned, exploited, twisted or destroyed by this force.

Our modern technological way of life is an immensely dramatic change from the vastly more earth-friendly modes of human existence that preceded this rapid global development for many thousands of years. It is a sad and unpopular fact that, as Western civilization has progressed, countless other civilizations have regressed, have indeed been ravaged and undone by the co-ercion of our own ideas and powers upon theirs. To this day, we either disregard the suffering of other cultures while continuing on our own path to global domination, or we view them through the eyes of sympathetic charity, regarding ourselves and our own culture as the superior and dominant people who will now help, aide, and assist these less fortunate people—whom we devastated in the first place—to acquire the modes of our own *elevated survival and sustenance.*

The deceptive hypocrisy of our impact upon, and subsequent response to, third world countries—the term "third world" ensuing from our own judgmental, self-centered, *superior,* and materialistic point of view—is confounded by our apparent lack of responsibility for our actions, both past and present, that have debilitated these peoples.

For instance, in Central and South America our oil production facilities have caused massive destruction to the land, obliterated livelihoods, and annihilated or deterred the lives of many indigenous peoples. In the mid-1990s, author Joe Kane documented the horrific impacts of corporate oil companies upon native cultures and the pristine Amazonian rainforest of Ecuador in his superbly written book *Savages.* In the book, Kane describes the struggle of one of the last remaining indigenous tribes—the Huaorani, who consider themselves to have not been conquered by the Western world—against the impending invasion of corporate oil.

Referencing his colleague Judith Kimerling, from her book *Amazon Crude,* Kane states: "In 1967 Texaco discovered commercial oil in the Oriente [the Ecuadorian rainforest]. In 1972 it completed a 312-mile pipeline from the Oriente to Ecuador's Pacific coast." From its inception until 1989, Kane continues, "the Texaco pipeline had ruptured at least twenty seven times, spilling 16.8 million gallons of raw crude ... most of it into the Oriente's delicate web of rivers, creeks and lagoons." As a firsthand witness to one of these colossal oil spills into the native Ecuadorian rainforest, Kane writes:

> While I was in Tonampare a valve in an oil well near the Napo broke, or was left open, and for two days and a night raw crude streamed into the river—at least 21,000 gallons and perhaps as many as 80,000, creating a slick that stretched from bank to bank for forty miles.

Due to this oil spill, a state of emergency was declared downstream in both Peru and Brazil; although, according to Kane, the oil company responsible for the spill disregarded the incident and did nothing to improve the situation. While in Ecuador, Kane visited various Huaorani communities and received firsthand reports of the extensive and extreme contamination of their water supplies by oil spills that had resulted in unruly health epidemics, severe illnesses, and deaths.

As if this were not bad enough, the problems of oil drilling extend beyond the awful impacts upon Huaorani and Indian health in general, as the settlements made by the oil companies result in drastic disruption, deviation, and desecration of traditional Indian culture. It is a complicated process because the imperialistic thrust of big oil coincides with the colonization, conversion to Christianity, and *re-education* of native Indians—in which, according to Kane, "no element of Huaorani culture was allowed to enter the curriculum." This enforced process of acculturation to Western ways results in the obliteration of the value, the history, and the very existence of traditional culture for all Indians affected.

During the months that Kane spent roaming through Ecuador, mainly with the Huaorani tribe, he experienced the traditional self-sufficient way of life that the Huaorani—along with many other indigenous South American tribes—have lived for millennia. After visiting colonized areas as well, he reports that Indians who have succumbed to a conversion to Western ways of living appear much worse off than those who have held to their traditional cultural patterns. Of these colonized and converted Huaorani, Kane writes:

> The people were dependent on goods brought in from outside, and many of them had become wage slaves to a culture they could never hope to be truly a part of—to a culture that, in fact, considered them little more than animals.

The convergence of the diverse aspects of capitalism, colonization, and conversion to Western ways and Christianity upon the various Indian tribes who are impacted all amounts to ethnocide. The fact that such corruption—initiated by Western imperialistic drives based on capitalistic gains—is still going on reveals that we have not progressed very far, at least globally speaking, in our path to becoming a more humane society.

REGRETTABLY, THE TYPICAL MODERN world citizen does not care much and has very little knowledge of the historical European conquests that have transformed spiritually and functionally intact cultures into materially indigent, chaotic, and violent third world countries. To the contrary, most of us are more or less plodding along our own *enlightened* paths of self-serving materialism. When we do give any consideration to cultures of a lesser material status, we judge and compare their "shabby" way of life to ours, in which running water, electricity, cars, central heating, air conditioning, and 24/7 hour grocery stores are essential.

We devalue indigenous and non-Western modes of living through our own ignorance and ingrained sense of superiority as we seek to *save* them, not by helping them to regain their own valued way of life, but by converting them to ours—which only reinforces our own paradigm of economic, technological, and religious superiority.

What we frequently fail to realize is that not every human being on this planet wants or needs to be hooked into the wave of technological progress with which we are so completely mesmerized. Not only does our enchantment with technology threaten our humanity, our society, and our planet, it also—through our continued pressures upon non-Western and non-technologically-based cultures to convert to the ways of the modern Western world—threatens to destroy the few remaining earth-based, indigenous peoples on this planet who would rather not be bothered by us or our materialistic lifestyles.

Do we really need to conquer the earth with our industrial and imperialistic capitalism until there is a 7-11 and McDonalds on every corner of the world? Until there are freeways chomping through every area of pristine land? Until all the forests have been chopped down and transformed into urban and industrial sprawl? Can't we contain ourselves with a little respect for the rest of the world?

Believe it or not, there are still people on this planet who enjoy living in the organic environment of nature—where electricity, motor vehicles, cells phones, online surfing, and iPods aren't necessities of life. They are able to survive and thrive quite well without all the modern accoutrements of modern life that we so desire—and many of them would like to remain as they are. Yet our attitude reveals an inner conviction that we have discovered the way of the future and must deliver this message *en force* to the rest of the world.

Rather than continuing on our present course aimed at a global takeover, we would benefit by asking ourselves what we can learn from non-Westernized cultures that still live in ancient and earth-honoring ways, cultures that we tend to brutalize and greedily destroy. It is only right that we learn to interact with these other cultures respectfully and humanely, allowing them their own way of life and sustenance upon this planet without interfering and coercing our interests and values upon them. Not everyone needs to drive a car on a freeway, work in an office, and live in a house in the city. In fact, if the seven billion+ human beings now alive on the planet all lived like this our environmental devastation would expand exponentially.

To expect a global conversion of all peoples in all places into an assimilation of our unique modern, technological way of life is not only stupid and supremely unreasonable; it is, essentially, insane. However, like a big, proud, arrogant peacock strutting itself all over the planet, the United States continues to engulf the globe with the gluttony of our capitalistic enterprises, all the while disregarding and disrupting the dignity of other countries, cultures, and peoples.

Reflecting on the impact of our very recent civilization upon other, much older, traditional and earth-based cultures, as well as the planet itself, we should notice and consider the damages we have done, the violence we have perpetrated, and the miseries we have created. We need to move beyond the Christian fantasy that we are a completely good and benign presence on the planet, that we are somehow God's chosen species with a free pass to do whatever we want regardless of the consequences. We should think about how we can be less egocentric and seek to balance our technological advances with tending to the well-being of the earth, other cultures, and one another. We should consider how to create more happiness and harmony in the world, and a little less profit.

Indeed, many individuals and organizations are becoming increasingly devoted to a greater consciousness of how to live in ways that are "earth friendly." Pro-environmental movements are coming to be known as "green" movements, and they provide good and necessary developments toward a future in which humans could be of greater benefit than detriment to the planet. However, very much work and change remains to be enacted in this area. Fortunately, our congress now appears to favor green philosophies and agendas towards transforming our industries and energy needs.

Although they are basically beneficial and restorative responses to the ills of a capitalist-driven industry, one inherent problem with environmental movements is that when we think about "saving the polar bears" or "saving the planet," we are still thinking abstractly. In truth, the planet was doing just fine before the advent of modern industry and technological society. Because we are the only threat to the planet and are only saving the planet from ourselves, slogans like "save the planet" really mean "stop the humans from destroying the planet."

Living our urban, fast-paced, and machine-based lives, very few of us have the time, energy, or ability to keep gardens, raise livestock, hunt for our sustenance, or otherwise live in any kind of experiential symbiosis with the planet. We live in suburban and citified concrete jungles where the animals have become cars, and the trees, forests, and waterfalls have become banks, department stores, and high rise apartment complexes.

Because we have created our own processed environment of roads, cars, industry, buildings, malls, and homes: an endless "urban sprawl" that houses an endless supply of manmade things; because we live in a world designed by capitalism, a world of incessant advertising, sales, and the desperate, frantic pursuit of material things—of production and products—a world molded and defined by radio, television, cyber computer devices, and the chronic bombardment of salesmen; we rarely, if ever, experience an intimate connection with the natural world, with the planet we are hoping "to save."

Sure we can learn all about the planet, discovering all sorts of marvelous things about the earth in science magazines or through viewing compelling video footage of nature; we can learn all about the planet in schools, in laboratories or other second hand means; but until we have a sustained, direct encounter with the earth and nature itself, how can we truly *know it*, and what will it ever really mean to us? And how few of us will ever accomplish this? Indeed, as it now stands our "civilization" is composed of a people and a culture that have moved out of nature into man-created worlds based upon the destruction of nature.

And this we call evolution ...

Ultimately, it's up to us to change the story, to write a new script, to realize who we are, what we have become, and to simply wake up to the realization of how we truly want the course of our lives and the life of our entire planet to unfold. So think about it, and let your thoughts permeate all that you do, for the existence of yourself and every other being around you may depend upon it.

III

THE MYTH OF THE INDIVIDUAL
& THE MECHANIZATION
OF THE BODY

A S A CHILD I PLAYED outside in the woods, fields, back-
yards, and back alleys. I loved to climb trees, ride my bike,
play ball, sled down hills during the winter, and generally
do fun stuff in the fresh air—where my body was active, my imagination inspired, and my senses engaged with the natural elements. These days, however, children spend most of their *free
time*, their *play time*, not outside playing, but inside sitting in
front of the computer, surfing the internet—where they email
friends, watch YouTube, and navigate through various profile
websites such as MySpace and Facebook. When they're not doing
that, they're usually watching television or playing video games.
In short, they inhabit a virtual universe which exists in another
dimension than the one in which I lived as a child. Sure, we
watched the television, but mostly after dark, and we had no digital reality to distract us from the wild outdoors during the day.

The focus of attention in adults, as well as children, is rapidly shifting from the natural world to the manmade world of electronic and cyber-infused technology—the media and related businesses are largely responsible for this transition as it turns us all into consumers off of which they bank huge profits. With this shift, however, the body has become much less engaged with life, and the rise in childhood, adolescent, and adult obesity is ever-escalating. Furthermore, children miss out on the grand adventures of rollicking through nature and encountering earthly mysteries.

When we ignore nature, we also ignore our bodies—probably because our bodies are the part of us that is most closely related to nature. Because we evolved through nature with the natural elements, we, *as bodies* and *as embodied souls*, need many kinds of interaction with nature to thrive. Our minds, however, are reorienting to the new, *disembodied*, technological world we are creating daily. So we have developed a kind of a mind-body split in ourselves wherein the body is more or less managed by the mind, and wherein reason has triumphed over instinct, thought over sensation, and mental activities over physical ones.

Within this modern paradigm, we take our bodies to the gym the same way we take our dog to the park, to exercise it because we want to stay *healthy*—even though the way we live the majority of our lives denies the natural health and freedom of the body. We're taught to maintain our bodies like we maintain our cars. We're told we must keep our bodies fit, trim, and muscular so that we will remain attractive to the opposite sex—or whatever sex interests us. We are basically programmed to manage the body rather than to truly inhabit it.

With our new strategic and tactical relationship to the body, there are excessive advertisements and commercials for surgical procedures and medicines that will alter our bodies in any way we desire: breast augmentations, liposuctions, and "male enhancement" products that will supposedly increase the size of a guy's erection—just to name a few. There are all kinds of surgeries to reduce the unwanted signs of aging on our bodies (because none of us really want to grow up), such as facelifts, Botox, and plastic surgery.

Yes, the mechanization of reality inflicted upon us by our modern and *evolved* society has taught us to treat our bodies with the impersonal affect of a busy clinical doctor, to degrade ourselves through constant objectification, to strip ourselves and our bodies of the dignity we deserve.

All these products and procedures demonstrate a preoccupation with perfecting the outer image of our body—in order to impress the outside world of society—not on enhancing or furthering our inner, subjective experience of our bodies or their potential for connecting us with the life-force. They are based on an objective *viewing* of the body and on a paradigm that emphasizes quantity—a long life—over quality—as in a life that is really worth living. There is something revolting about the media constantly instructing me on how to manipulate and change my body so that it is somehow more socially acceptable and "society-approved," while simultaneously disregarding the reality that my body is my most intimate locus of experience.

These images of the *ideal body* are like images of the ideal car, or the ideal lover, forever imploring us to keep ourselves looking shiny, young, athletic, and genitally well-endowed. The media, the salesmen, the doctors, and the body-manipulation scientists would have us contort ourselves into images of super-humans, all the while laughing themselves silly to the bank.

THE MECHANIZATION OF THE BODY entails that we first begin to kill its spirit and its soul. Modern society accomplishes this by housing our bodies incessantly, from the school classroom to the work office to the living room to the car. Our bodies have become like animals in the zoo. Our mind, as the enforcer of this way of life, is like the farmer, while our poor body is the hapless farm animal who is corralled and kept all day in a barn. As such, we have instituted a system of education, as well as many modes of employment, that are degrading to the body and to the freedom of one's spirit. Thus, we have become addicted to distilled spirits as an easily available alternative to a truly spiritually fulfilling life.

To understand the profound impact of our way of life it must be remembered that, until relatively very, very recently in the overall life and evolution of the human species, we were a mobile creature, interacting directly with the living, natural environment in which we existed. We hunted and gathered, planted and harvested, and worked and played with the natural world for the majority of our lives.

Now, from early childhood, we are locked inside school classrooms that resemble jails—in both form and function. We are removed from the natural world where we once learned real skills that taught us how to survive and to appreciate the planet, and "educated" through a process of learning mostly abstract knowledge. As children, we are required to repress our impulses for activity and exploration, and forced to focus on mainly conceptual and verbal modes of information via endless discourse and books. In this process the body is degraded as some secondary thing that is not worthy of a primary focus—whose instincts and sexuality must be strictly curtailed and tamed in order for us to fit in with the grand production of society.

For many of us, the twelve to twenty years of *education* we receive train us to withstand entire adult lives of working on abstract projects in offices where we continue to repress our natural bodily instincts to interact with the world and, instead, focus exclusively on the capabilities of our minds—which to a large degree have become an unfulfilling mental process divorced from the body.

We know something is wrong with living like this, and deep down we feel hopeless and resentful that *this is just the way things are*. But what the hell can we do about an inherited systematic social structure and mode of reality that is crammed down our throats from the moment we are born?

IF WE ARE EQUATING SURVIVAL with suffering, and work with energy exerted, perhaps we have made less progress in the last five hundred to five thousand years than we like to believe that we have. Yes, we are more sheltered from the elements and we tend to live longer lives. But does living in a box engaged in either repetitive and dull physical labor such as factory work, or the abstract processing of virtual information and administrative orders involved with office work surpass, or even compare to, the "primitive life" in which we directly experienced and engaged the vast and infinite natural world, and in which we felt intrinsically connected to Mother Earth and Father Sky?

These concepts may sound silly and antiquated to our modern, enlightened, and superior sensibility, but in times past they were more than just concepts, they were living realities which most of us have lost the ability or inclination to perceive.

In times past, before the advent of modernity and technological culture, human beings maintained an integral relationship to the earth, the elements, animals, plants, and overall ecology. In these times, we lived as part of an interactive and organic reality in which we were embedded with an experiential and profound sense of belonging to our community and to the earth and cosmos as the origins of our lives. Hunting and gathering was a way of life in which for humans to survive we learned to experience a very intimate sense of interrelatedness with the environment.

Through living in such close contact with the planet, we knew we belonged to Her in all Her incredible variety and display. Earth-based and earth-friendly cultures do not relate to the earth on a mainly conceptual plane, as we do now; nor do they think or act as if the earth belonged to them, as do we. And as far as I know, they do not experience the *crisis in belonging*, the monumental sense of alienation, loneliness, and isolation that we of the modern world do. In fact, such cultures still exist to this day and are not only a relic of the past, although we rarely hear about them in a true and redeeming light.

These days, as many of us live in huge metropolis cities, our sense of belonging is distant and fleeting at best. Our crisis of belonging, or of not belonging, extends beyond the workplace to the greater society, and in many cases composes our essential identity as a form of trauma upon our souls.

In the United States, throughout the 20th and 21st centuries, our sense of identity has also been shaped and molded by the concept of the "rugged individual," the Marlboro Man, Clint Eastwood, John Wayne sort of hyper-masculine guy. The idea of the autonomous, liberated, enterprising individual who doesn't really need anything from anyone else that he cannot acquire through efforts of his own ambitions is complicit with the imperialistic vision with which the Western powers have gradually conquered the planet.

This rugged individual may be depicted as an imperialistic conqueror, a sort of hero archetype who we see portrayed continually in movies as the good guy reigning victorious over the bad guy. In actual life, however, not only do we see the rugged individual in a positive light, as the genius millionaire such as Bill Gates who has risen above the detritus of the common man; we also see him in his darkened, shadow form as the demented, violent criminal through such figures as Charles Manson and the Unabomber who attacked and devastated the very communities in which they lived. The rugged individual, whether characterized as good or evil, is moreover defined by his or her battles *against the world* than by how he or she fits in with the human community or experiences a sense of belonging in any nurturing or loving way.

Most of us, in comparison to the indigenous, non-Western person, have a diminished sense of belonging to the community or family in which we live. As rugged individuals, we have all become conditioned to be primarily responsible for ourselves, expected to meet our own needs, to "fend for ourselves," and to thereby prove our strength and abilities, thus our worth, to the world. Though we may have been liberated from some of the oppressions of the tribe—such as the supposed "groupthink"—we have also suffered a good deal of psychological dismemberment and isolation in our newfound freedom.

In actuality, most of us barely know our neighbors and are usually less interested in knowing them than we already do. *A stranger is not someone who we do not know; a stranger is someone who we do not want to know.* And in this modern, densely populated world we have become a culture of strangers, motivated through social instructions and government intimidations to actually fear one another. Meanwhile, our overemphasis on technological devices—in the next awesome electronic or cyber product—isolates us from the natural world, instilling us with an overeagerness for entirely man-made forms of stimulation or entertainment.

WE LIVE IN A FURY, like a wave constantly breaking into an anticipated future of the promised land, as if we existed in a time zone ahead of ourselves. We thrive on adrenalin, excitement, and perpetual stimulation from our man-made, technological inventions. Many of us spend hours every day mesmerized in a mental-visual engagement with our computers—the new TV—and their seemingly limitless sources of information, whether at work, where many of our duties may entail extensive interactions on the computer or internet, or in the realm of our personal relationships, where we create profile hubs of potential interactions with other virtual reality explorers on MySpace or Facebook.

Yet in reality, we remained more estranged from one another than ever.

Developing enlarged egos helps us to compensate for this painful condition. Getting a great education, a degree, and a great job with great pay gives us the credentials we need to feel like an important person. But feeling important is not a good substitute for feeling loved, accepted, valued, and intrinsically connected and interrelated with the greater web of humankind and the planet at large. Many individuals at the height of success, having attained the perfect image of the self-actualized materialist man, are in actuality quite lonely, conflicted in their human relationships, devoid of spirituality or connection to a greater source than their own capitalist-driven egos, and empty of true inner fulfillment.

Or so I'm told ...

IV

HUMAN *BEING* OR HUMAN *GOING?*

"We're so engaged in doing things to achieve purposes of outer value that we forget that the inner value, the rapture that is associated with being alive, is what it's all about."
~Joseph Campbell, *The Power of Myth*

A S HUMAN *BEINGS* LIVING in the modern world, we must ask ourselves, "How does our *being* coexist with all our *going?*" It's an important question because every day we are constantly and simultaneously moving in multiple directions so rapidly that we rarely have the opportunity to connect with the *being* of our human nature. *Being* is not the same as *doing*, and we live in a culture of non-stop acceleration, of continual, frenzied, anxiety and competition-driven, *on the go* action.

Even our foremost pastimes, the movies, television shows, and sporting events we view—things we do to recover from all our work and busyness—exemplify this glorification of non-stop, nerve-riveting action, of violence, crime, sexual exploits, and destruction.

In this world, there is very little time for rest and relaxation, and when there is time we virtually recoil from it in horror, somehow believing that the moment we cease to act, we also cease to exist. Thus, our most revered and apparent sense of self is identified with anxiety and accomplishment. Many of us tend to resolve this predicament, albeit temporarily, by sedating ourselves with drugs and/or alcohol. When the work day is done the only way many people can *change gears* or get relaxed is to crack open the bottle or load up the pipe. Our use of mind-altering substances also displays our need to return to the *being* of our human nature; so why does our normal modern mode of living have to operate in antithesis to it?

By losing regular contact with our underlying non-anxiety driven, non-neurotic, but intrinsically stable, calm, and reflective inner nature, we have ceased to function as, or find fulfillment in, the inherent human *being* that we are. Indeed, we are becoming increasingly like the programmed devices with which our technological society inundates us, giving the outer impression of vast and dynamic possibilities, but moreover removed from the human heart. Because we lack a true connection with our *inner being,* we are terrified of being alone or of being at rest. Paradoxically, through our compulsive obsessions with the frenetic, technology-driven pace of life: *we have alienated ourselves from ourselves.*

The more we aspire to be *in touch* with each other via technological devices such as the cell phone, internet, and webcam, the further we stray from the simple human capacity to share space: to talk in person face to face, to be silent, to listen, to breath the same air, to break bread, to live closely together, and to feel the true embodied companionship of those we love, of family, friends, and even strangers. Having quantifiably more *contacts* in our cell phone, MySpace, or Facebook account is not the same as having more quality relationships that incorporate depth and richness. Sometimes "less is more," but that's something our capitalistic, money-driven society does not easily grasp.

In the modern Western world, powerful personalities are not usually measured as such by their magnitude of loving-kindness or their propensity to inspire the imagination and the human spirit—although figures such as John Lennon and Martin Luther King, Jr. certainly were—but moreover by their capacity to control others, to manipulate the markets and accumulate wealth. In the world of capitalism, the way powerful people relate to things, such as time, or even other people, is not in any way contemplative, reflective or appreciative; it is almost completely manipulative, aimed at molding things to fit in with their goals of how they want the world to be—for them, "time is money."

Many of us, especially powerful people, actually value our manipulations of machines over our human relationships, and over activities or engagements that do not involve machines, like reading a book, taking a walk, or watching a sunset. The living spirit inside us was not made by a machine, neither was the sun, nor the sky, nor the earth. But the way we live denotes that machines are more significant than any of these things, and such a way of life neglects our opportunities for truly *being* human.

Why, in our modern world, is *going* valued so utterly and completely over *being*? Why, indeed, is *being* so profoundly devalued, held in high suspicion, and looked upon as idleness and laziness? Because if one is simply *being*—simply enjoying *being* alive, *being* human, *being* in time and space, *being* a human *being*—then one is not contributing to the slavish wheel of commerce, one is not feeding the grand capitalist scheme with one's time and energy, with one's blood, sweat, and tears, or with one's very life.

In the state of being, we cannot be accounted for by the measuring sticks of materialism.

Going makes money, *being* has no need for it. *Going* needs to be fueled by saleable items like gasoline and coffee, doughnuts and cell phones, CDs and computers; *being* needs no fuel, its fuel is the acceptance and appreciation of whatever exists in this moment. *Going* has many goals and agendas that require much effort and activity to accomplish. *Being* has only one goal: to *be*. In a state of *being*, just *being* is enough.

"What the hell are you talking about!?!" you exclaim, jumping out of your seat. "What is this *being* of which you speak?!?" In the modern world, there is an unacknowledged social consensus that we should always be preoccupied with some form of outside stimulation, that we are forever in need of something we don't have—we've become chronic "channel-surfers" of life. That's why we're always *going*. We can't relax. Most of us can't just sit with ourselves for five seconds.

In a state of *being*, however, we have the opportunity to notice what we are experiencing without reactively and automatically pursing our attachments, cravings, or desires. In a state of *being*, we are able to notice what our minds are thinking, and what our bodies are feeling. We are able to notice, or sense internally, the sensations inside our own skin and our perceptions of the world around us, as well as how it feels to simply *be* in the world. Attunement to your *being* is the same thing as becoming aware of your *presence:* the spirit, force, energy, or whatever you would call the *essence* of who and what you are as a living, sentient *human being*.

Although *being* is shared by all humans of all cultures and all eras, and by all living creatures, in truth, *being* as an aspect of our human condition and potential is not a reinforced or celebrated capacity in modern Western culture. Because we focus so exclusively on *going* and on *becoming*, you could say that *being* is not an innately modern Western phenomenon or faculty. Therefore, it is somewhat strange for us to consider. In fact, b*eing* is more well known to pre-Western, indigenous, and Eastern cultural paradigms in which humans co-exist more directly with the planet and with one another. *Being* implies a sense of profound interconnection and interrelationship with the social and natural world, involving not only one's mental processes but also one's body awareness, sensations, energies, instincts, and intuitions.

ACCORDING TO HISTORICAL ACCOUNTS, when European colonialists came to the American continent, they tended to view the Native Americans as lazy and lacking in ambition. In his recent book, *Tree of Rivers: The Story of the Amazon*, John Hemming quotes the French scientist La Condamine, from 1743, as having described Amazonian natives as "Enemies of work, indifferent to all motives of glory, honour or gratitude; solely concerned with the immediate object ... with no care for the future; and incapable of foresight or reflection."

Obviously, time enlarges perspective, and we know today that during the brutal conquest of the Americas, the European mindset differed so radically from the Native American's that gross misjudgments and racial prejudices were made. Commenting on this situation from the other side of the looking glass, the Native American medicine man Lame Deer states in his autobiography:

> Because we refuse to step out of our reality into this frogskin illusion, [his term for capitalism] we are called dumb, lazy, improvident, immature, other-worldly. It makes me happy to be called 'other-worldly,' and it should make you so. It's a good thing our reality is different from theirs.

Both these accounts, the first discriminatory and the second revelatory, imply another way of relating to time within the Native American culture in which—unlike our modern Western model which is bound to the clock—it appears that *being* is as equally valued as *going*. Denoting this *other kind of time*, the poet Juan Ramon Jimenez wrote, "More time is not more eternity." Thus, from the poet's perspective time is a subjective experience, closely related to one's particular *state of being*.

Similarly, from *The Labyrinth of Solitude*, the Mexican poet Octavio Paz states, "the conception of time as a fixed present and as pure actuality is more ancient than that of chronometric time, which is not an immediate apprehension of the flow of reality but is instead a rationalization of its passing." He goes on to describe "original time," which "coincides with our inner, subjective time," in which one's "subjective life becomes identical with exterior time, because this has ceased to be a spacial measurement and has changed into a source, a spring, in the absolute present, endlessly recreating itself."

These descriptions of time are certainly different from the ways in which we are conditioned to conceptualize, and thus experience, time in modern Western society. Time as "pure actuality," and as "a source ... in the absolute present" connotes *time as being* and as *presence*, as the flowing of life, and as the flow through which we encounter existence. Experiencing time in this manner relates to the context and process of our lives, as well as the contents. In this mode of reality, by virtue of containing and underlying our experience, time becomes the ocean and ground of our *being*, and—through having been returned to its a priori or transcendent function—loses exclusive identification with *going*.

One way to illustrate the experience of *being*, not in chronological or linear time, but in this other, magical or eternal time, is to recall a time when you were *in love*. For love has always been an experience that somehow takes us out of the ordinary mode of mundane time as experienced by mortals, and into the realm of angels who live in mythological time. At such a time, and in such a *state of being*, the love you shared with the other person felt like the truest, most profound fulfillment of your life, of your entire *being*. What you did or where you were *going* didn't matter, because you were in love, and in that *state of being* all your pressing concerns with the world faded away ... for a while.

It could be that something other than *being in love* takes you to a *state of being*, wherein you are completely absorbed and fulfilled without having to *go* anywhere else or accomplish anything. Simple everyday rituals like having a cup of coffee and gazing out the window at a beautiful landscape can induce our appreciation for being. There are also a variety of awareness disciplines, such as meditation, that provide practical techniques for developing one's reflective awareness and appreciation of being. Being as a quality of experience can be cultivated in many activities, even washing the dishes.

Creative activities—like painting, dancing, playing music, or writing—induce states of *being in action* that, once engaged, seem to take us over, to transport us effortlessly into another *state of being* in which our capacity to experience and express our human identity and potential is profoundly intensified, expanded, and illuminated. Though we may end up with some kind of a finished product, such as a book, poem, song, or performance piece, the essential aspect of the activity involves a creative, or otherwise unnamable, transformation in the interior quality of our state of *being*, which then becomes manifest as an external accomplishment.

THE POINT HERE IS NOT that modern technology and its advancements are implicitly wrong or bad for us—though that may ultimately prove to be true—but that becoming entranced with them to the exclusion of our true human nature, our inherent humanness, is a problem. It is both ignorant and dangerous to focus only on the outer world we have created and not the inner worlds that compose who we are. And yet how can we remain connected to the inner world of our essential selves when our very civilization is based on the domination and manipulation of human beings, as well as nature itself?

Our current thrust of technology and perpetual states of rapid social activity—in the name of progress—has a two-fold effect: the first is the internal eclipsing of our capacity for *being*, the second is the external eradication of nature—the native environment in which we are most truly human. Through social engineering—gradually eliminating both our internal and external reference points for who we instinctually are as human *beings*—society remakes us into creatures who think, feel, and behave in the ways they want us to.

How do we address such insidious problems that are so deeply embedded in the function, structure, and foundations of our society that they compose the basis and overall effect of how we live? For most of us, it is nearly impossible to conceive of another perspective or way of living that does not entail the continual subjugation of nature, alongside the never-ending build-up and harnessing of technological forms of human preoccupation that guide us away from our inner selves. How can we live simultaneously in a machine-based world and on a nature-based planet? Isn't such a way of life an inherent contradiction forecasting an imminent demise?

Currently our machines, our industry, and our technology are not only eclipsing our souls, they are killing nature. Because we are not machines, because we are of the earth, and because we are also nature, our machine-based way of life is also killing us.

If we are to find solutions other than an unconscious global suicide and apocalypse, we will find them not through a crescendo of our current maniacal mode of reactive action, but through a more reflective attuning of our *human being* to the *being of the world*. Perhaps in tending to the world—through our own *con-*

scious beings as opposed to our *unconscious goings*—we can effect a healing in which we will discover the reality of the anima mundi, the soul of the world that, like us, is also alive. Through this deeper connection based on spiritual recognition, we can initiate more sensitive, aware, and unifying interactions within ourselves, with one another, and with the planet whose *being* is also essentially part of ours.

V

CULTURE OF LOST SOULS
IN SEARCH OF A PROFIT

IN THE UNITED STATES, our *raison d'être*—our underlying ethic and principle of living—is that of *profit and progress*, which we continually pursue through industry, technology, and capitalism. Through these prevailing forms we are intent on invading and gleaning of its potential material worth every nook and cranny of nature, every possible "resource" we can access. After nearly obliterating the native cultures that dwelled here before our arrival, we've proceeded by continually "clearing land," a misleadingly positive sounding term which really means chopping down trees and plants, flora and fauna, leveling the uneven natural surfaces of the earth and *implanting* roads, housing developments, shopping centers, and gas stations—all the basic substrates of our material society. In this way, we are recklessly ever-encroaching upon the sanctity of the earth.

Like all societies and cultures, we need to survive. But why can't we integrate ourselves more harmoniously into the encompassing natural environment? (Probably for the same reason that we didn't integrate ourselves more peaceably into the existing *human environment* that was here on this continent when we first arrived.) Traditional Japanese and Native American cultures have some idea of this, which we are lacking. Not only does our greed know no limits, but the modern civilization into which we are transforming the natural earth is increasingly becoming a mechanical hodge-podge of repetitive, soulless, and uninspired dreck.

Why do we no longer infuse the design of our towns and the structures of our dwellings with the same sort of sensibility and beauty with which nature grows plants, trees, hills, and landscapes? It appears as a sort of calamity of ugliness when homes are built side by side like boxes in a row that all look alike. In Southern California this way of habitation is the norm; they call them "tract homes." This form of bulk community housing development is built under the same premise as a Wal-Mart or Sam's Club; by providing a lower quality mass-market home which more people can afford, contractors increase their profits through an amplification of the principle of quantity.

An extension of *the rule of sameness and monotony* displayed in tract homes is also found in the construction of strip malls, which have become the rule of thumb, the latest fashion in our mortification of culture in the United States. Especially in the newer towns, there is the same conglomeration of stores, shops, and fast food restaurants, all mass produced and plastered together in a similar anti-artistic form. There appears to be no originality in this kind of construction, either in design, form, or content, as they are built only to satisfy the consumer demands of ease and efficiency.

You may as well not go to the next town because it looks just like the one you came from. This kind of "township" is really a desecration of the human spirit of creativity, an assault on the senses, and an abomination of aesthetics. Of course, as long as we're getting the things we want—coffee, grub, videos, and mani-cures—we all appear to be just as happy as ever.

Over the years, in the United States we have traded form for function. Think about that for a minute. Although we have gained considerably in the area of accessibility to products and services, we have lost sorely in the area of beauty and style, aes-thetics that are more important to our creative *soul nature* than the construction workers or the bankers seem to understand.

You can see this process clearly in the production of cars. Up until sometime in the mid-70s, cars were made with a flair for design, as a true craft with attention to the eye; like pieces of wood carved into totems, furniture, or works of art, cars resem-bled art as sculptures of steel and leather that engaged the heart with the magnificence of their form, velocity, and power.

These days, and for some good reason, cars are made primarily to meet standards of fuel efficiency and comfort. They're also made out of cheaper materials, mainly plastics instead of steel. However, the typical modern car—like the modern house and the modern strip mall—fails to inspire. For the sake of efficiency, ease, and affordable low-cost production, we have sacrificed the style, aesthetic beauty, and artistry which once composed our cars, homes, and the towns in which we live.

These days everything we do as a society boils down to the profit margin, where the bottom line is the dollar bill, not the soul or our aesthetic sensibilities and inherent appreciation of form. Because the particular and affecting qualities of person, place, and thing have become so greatly diminished, verily, life has ceased to impress us as dearly or as profoundly as it once did.

To ignore the significance of form is to deny the reality that the world around us, the sensate world—the physical, palpable world of forms—affects us so profoundly that it is truly a part of who we are, *the aspect of ourselves in which we live.* Without the world, there would be no self. Therefore, in some basic, primal sense *the world in which we live is also the world which lives inside us.* Herein lies the vital importance of our shaping the world in which we live.

When we create a world of carelessly constructed ticky-tack—cars, buildings, houses, schools, and offices that are utterly uninteresting and unappealing to the eye—we must remember that our perceptual and sensation-based interactions with these environments intimately affect our inner experience and being, belittling our penchant, our thirst, our need for beauty and our capacity for imagination. It also insults the instinctual nature inside us which is inherently interrelated with the same cosmic force responsible for the infinitely creative productions of nature.

Do we, as the harbingers of evolution, and as the self-proclaimed emissaries of God and the natural world, not have a responsibility, a duty, to co-create a world within the world of nature that at least strives to maintain a par with the excellence, the amazing revelatory elegance, and delight-inspiring display that She has created? When we make ugly environments in which we live, we are demeaning our God-given place in this beautiful world of nature. Isn't the idea of living well to make the world a better place, to "add unto and multiply" the beauty, the miracle of this living world we have inherited?

Ancient cultures seemed to have understood this. Look at the fortresses of Machu Picchu, Grecian statues and relics, the Taj Majal, and the Seven Wonders of the World. Or simply recall the Gothic cathedrals of medieval Europe. In times past, we Americans devoted ourselves to creating things of beauty as well. We used to invest more time, energy, thought, and love into our labors and crafts—just look at 19th Century furniture or the Victorian homes and buildings of long-established cities.

These days everything is made as quickly as possible with the main goal of profit—the primary tenet of our capitalism. Our current culture produces a limitless supply of crappily mass-produced ticky-tack at an astronomical rate so that profit may be maintained and ever-increased. We also produce garbage and dumps as equally fast. According to the Clean Air Council, in the United States "4.39 pounds of trash per day and up to 56 tons of trash per year are created by the average person."

We now live in a disposable world, using then throwing away most of the things we buy with extreme rapidity. Just go to the local dump or look at the enormous loads of trash that are shipped to Africa and Asia where materially indigent citizens pick through all we've discarded because we wanted the next, the newest, and best thing. The practices of our disposable culture reveal an inner assumption that the world is viewed as a limitless supply of raw materials and goods which exist primarily for our own exploit and plunder. Because the things we use are so disposable, so easily replaced, we lack a sense of value for them, and therefore treat them, and their sources, without much respect or care.

Why did we come to adopt such a disposable way of life in which our valuing of the world has become so greatly diminished? Perhaps it is related to our increasing demand for instant gratification. "In the old days," as people like to say, "things were made to last," not just the objects we used, but also our relationships—our marriages and friendships with other human beings.

Perhaps part of the answer to the question of disposability lies in the increasingly capitalistic nature of our economy, wherein it seems everyone is trying to sell you something, and in which we, the common citizens, have been reduced to mere "consumers." In cahoots with capitalism's obsession with *profit* is technology's obsession with *progress*, in which we must continually update and improve products, such as computers and cars, so that they become more enticing for purchase by the consumer. In this way, our *culture of civilization* influences a forward-looking mode of operation in which the past and nature are both devalued—for us, nature and technology are antithetical, as nature is equated with the past, which we tend to ignore, and technology is equated with the future, towards which we eagerly stream. You're just not hip if you don't have a new car, a new humungous flat screen TV, and a brand new iPod, iPad, or iPhone.

In pre-Western cultures, such as those of the Native Americans, the focus of society was not only mindful of the future in which, according to the Iroquois, "In every deliberation, we must consider the impact on the seventh generation ... even if it requires having skin as thick as the bark of a pine," but also, in a more balanced manner, upon the present *as inherited from the past*, including longstanding traditions and ceremonies, as well as a tendency to venerate the aged elders for their wealth of experience and collected wisdom.

In contrast, our disposable society holds little veneration for the past, for tradition, for the collected wisdom of its elders, or for nature. "Out with the old and in with the new!" is our ever-raging motto, a sentiment that also celebrates the cult of youth which is glorified in modern America.

How, you may ask, can we blame technology and capitalism for our disposable society and devaluation of nature? Because, in a world that can be bought and sold, we replace the inherent value of life and nature with our own superimposed man-made materialistic values that stem from our aforementioned priorities. We cease to see that a thing—a tree, river, field of wheat, flower, or even a person—retains a unique value in and of itself, a value and an essential reality that cannot ever be bought or sold because it is a reality that man did not and cannot create.

We automatically translate the *reality* of the natural world into a *meaning* created by humankind—for the sole purpose of benefiting humankind. Thereby, we fail to see the larger picture of our human existence within the context of nature.

Consumed by our own selfish concerns and narcissistic desires, we lose connection, empathy, and understanding for the natural world around us. In this way, we become blind to the reality and significance of the natural world in which we live. Thus our thinking becomes distorted as well, and we come to act in ways which demonstrate our belief that this entire terrestrial planet exists only for the benefit and greater glory of humans. Yet, in this belief, we are simply wrong, as it is just this kind of thinking which has contributed to the devastation of the world around us and, increasingly, to our own self-destruction as well.

Our greatest failure as human beings in the modern world is that we've come to believe we live in a sort of vacuum, wherein we've forgotten the ancient teaching of the Buddha, that *all things are truly interconnected.*

IN THEORY, CAPITALISM MAY APPEAR to be a good method of economy, though in practice it often times causes great harm. One reason for this is that the way in which we practice capitalism does not tend to incorporate morals or ethics. Many would say it is unethical to tear down hunks of pristine rainforest, whether in the Pacific Northwest or the Amazon—which in Central and South America has entailed the decimation of entire tribes of people, horrific harm, and extinction of many animal and plant species, as well as irreversible devastation to vast ecosystems—yet even to this day these practices go on so that enterprising capitalists can continue to fatten their cash wad.

The bottom line of capitalism has become the translation of any product or service into dollar bills, into the abstract meaning of money which enables the capitalist to procure greater wealth and status in the material society. It is a never-ending cycle that all too often has absolutely no heart or humanity in it. There is a reason we refer to money as "cold hard cash." Cash is *cold* and *hard*. It freezes the heart and blinds the eyes. Because of this, we desperately need to infuse our capitalist and material pursuits with a more compassionate set of ethical practices.

Of course, there are many small-time business-people supporting themselves and their families without hurting, or intending to hurt, others. Most of us struggle just to tread water in the choppy seas of our debts and obligations. We work long hard hours, and should be rewarded and benefited for our labors. I do not dispute this whatsoever. What bothers me is when certain individuals earn unnecessarily vast amounts of money at the tragic expense of others. This sort of behavior has been termed "cannibalism" because it feeds off the labor and lives of less materially or socially powerful peoples, and may be wholly destructive to both natural habitats and entire cultures of people.

In his powerful and alarmingly honest account of the impact of European colonialism upon the American continent, *Columbus and other Cannibals*, Jack D. Forbes defines cannibalism as *"the consuming of another's life for one's own private purpose or profit."* (Italics his.) He goes on to state, *"imperialism and exploitation are forms of cannibalism and, in fact, are precisely those forms of cannibalism which are most diabolical or evil ..."*

All too often, the modern practice of capitalism incorporates cannibalistic tendencies which degrade both people and planet. Only by identifying this process—when and where it happens—and seeking to rectify it, can we potentially heal the damages done.

An example of such cannibalism can be seen in Chile, where the global thrust of capitalism, via logging companies, is met with resistance by native tribes struggling to retain their traditional way of life. In an article entitled "Chile's Battleground of Culture vs. Profit," Tim Vandenack describes this difficult situation:

> Through most of the 19th century, the Mapuches [a native tribe] held dominion over an area covering 20,000

square miles of south central Chile. But government expropriations, colonization, and land deals the Mapuches say took advantage of their unfamiliarity with the Spanish language and the Chilean legal system have whittled that to 1,200 square miles on scattered plots in the area. ... Marcelo Martini, head of the [logging company] in Temuco, says "The Mapuches' main problem is extreme poverty ... The Mapuches have lower literacy, employment, and income levels than Chile's overall population ... training and education are key so that they can get well-paying jobs in the mainstream economy, with logging companies or other enterprises." While acknowledging the need for more education, Mapuche leaders reject assimilation. "If we all become logging company workers or professionals, we lose our cultural identity and the essence of what it is to be a Mapuche," says Mr. Nain [a Mapuche Indian leader].

The problem here is modern day capitalism's tendency to *bulldoze* over other forms of culture, sustenance, and economy. Notice how the leader of the logging company suggests that the solution to the conflict is for the native Indians to simply become educated so they can get jobs working for the logging company! Of course, this is a complex issue as loggers need to eat too. However, whenever one group infringes itself upon another, negating the other group's ability to survive, the question of appropriate boundaries, ethics, and rights must be raised.

An overriding question may be: "can these two modes of living—the ancient and the modern—ever harmoniously co-exist?" Or will the modern powers continue to subvert, dominate, and eradicate the ancient cultures? This last question could also be paraphrased as: "Will technology and capitalism continue to overcome and defeat the earth, until the earth has been irreparably mutilated?"

Ironically, through our efforts to procure the money needed to devise a "better and more developed world" for ourselves, we often sacrifice those very qualities of life that we most value, and which, ostensibly, our new and improved society was designed to engender in the first place. Qualities and conditions such as sanity, peace of mind, happiness, harmonious relationships with others, getting enough sleep, rest and relaxation, being creatively engaged, having adequate physical exercise, enough time for satisfying artistic self-expression, a sense of security and safety, and a compassionate, respectful work environment.

Could it be that we are caught up in a self-destructive loop? Although a few of us do truly enjoy our work, more often than not we feel burnt out by our jobs, assaulted by our bills and *the cost of living*, and spend much of our existence clamoring just to earn enough cash to keep the vultures at bay.

One has only to look at images of Wall Street or the rush hour madness of any given city for a glimpse into the mad world of earning a living. At every turn it seems there is another bill to pay—whether it's car repair, credit cards, taxes, illnesses and accidents, even a night out on the town, or just the general upkeep of our status quo. And, if that wasn't enough, we are constantly accosted by commercials and advertisements on how to spend more money!

The very nature of living in a capitalistic world is that we are constantly exposed to *more things and more opportunities* that we are continuously harassed to procure, thereby indebting ourselves through payment plans, credit cards, and financing which is repaid with interest.

There is something about being constantly, incessantly assaulted by people who want my money that is insulting and demeaning to the dignity and condition of being alive. I can't walk two feet in this world without being encouraged to purchase something—I am the constant prey of predator-humans.

Capitalism exalts the survival instinct into an ultimately grotesque and monstrous reality, a dark foreboding fog with a glittering neon lining that is ever-threatening to devour you.

And yet, we seem to be the happiest and most excited when we've got "money to burn," at the mall or shopping center—or now, simply online—where we are empowered by our cash or credit card, finally freed from the oppressive chains of the workplace and rewarded with the freedom to purchase some marvelous thing that helps to justify, or compensate for, the long, endless hours we spend in our mortifying pursuits to *earn a living.*

Compared to other leading industrial countries around the world, the United States ranks rather high in the average number of hours worked, a little under 1,800 per year, or about 34 hours per week. A few countries rank higher than us, among them Mexico and Japan; however, Korea tops the charts at almost 2,400 hours per year, which is nearly 46 per week. Canada and every European nation work less hours than do we—France and Germany average about 1,350 hours per year, or a little under 26 hours per week. Europe's lower number of hours worked is probably due to their tendency toward longer paid vacations, a standard of 4-6 weeks per year, as opposed to the United States' standard of 2-3 weeks per year.

In high contrast, the !Kung Bushmen, an indigenous hunter-gatherer tribe of the African Kalahari desert, work somewhere around two and a half days per week for about 6 hours per day, which equals approximately 15 hours per week and 780 hours per year.

As they say, all work and no play makes Jack a dull boy...

Sadly, most of us are held hostage by the ongoing cycle of work, pay, and debt. It goes something like this: we work hard, get burnt out, get paid, buy something to compensate for feeling burnt out, incur more bills, and then must work harder to pay the bills.

See the cycle?

Many of us are deeply trapped in this cycle. But this is what capitalism wants; this, we're convinced, creates a good, healthy economy. (It also creates job security for employers who need to keep their employees working for them like indentured servants so that profits and progress can be maintained.) But does this way of life create good, healthy, and happy citizens, families, and societies?

Capitalism and technology are economic-based functions of our modern culture that support our definitions and understanding of who we are as a collective humanity. Although we take their existence for granted as essential, unalterable aspects of our society, they both must transform from their present focus on material profit and progress, to more sustainable, inclusive, and spiritual goals, embodying values that acknowledge our unity as human beings with the entire planet—values such as beauty, compassion, and interconnection, in which caring for one another replaces our incessant drives for competition.

Profit and progress need to be redefined in more internally referenced or spiritual ways—as in *profitable* emotional or psychological states that *progress* our feelings of well-being—rather than exclusively in terms of materiality, commerce, and production. In an increasingly holistic world, we must realize that there is more to life than material advancements.

Jesus Christ said: "What shall it profit a man if he gains the whole world but loses his soul?"

It is my belief that *the basis of human life is the experience of the soul,* through which we come to grasp the miracle of being alive, which neither profit nor progress can ever change.

VI

THE SHORT HAIRS

WHY DO ALL MALE POLITICIANS, all male news-casters, bankers, and policemen have short hair?

What is this unspoken, unarticulated taboo against men—especially middle to upper class, professional, and media-vised men—having any hair that can be seen below their ears?

What perceived anti-male threat is to be found in the miraculous substance of hair?

What secret terror of hair do men carry around that keeps them bound like slaves to the metal shears of the haircutter?

Why is it only okay for a man of social significance to have longer hair if he is a musician, an artist, or a black linebacker?

Outside of a very few exceptions, why is it that modern manhood—especially socially powerful and materially affluent images of manhood—appears to be defined by a necessary preclusion and an overall lack and abandonment of any kind of hair style that exceeds more than an inch or two in length?

Even most upwardly-mobile female professionals, especially politicians, have closely cropped "bob" hairdos, as if they are attempting to keep in line with the professional *man's world* of short hair.

Maybe this taboo against long hair explains why society has compensated modern man with fantasies of a penis enlargement—as evidenced by all-night infomercials on such magical products. His animal hair, his beautiful, powerful, sexual hair has been decapitated, has been castrated by the mainstream social mores of the short-haired, short-tempered, narrow-minded, and small-hearted imperialistic man. One has only to look as far as the story of Samson & Delilah for an accurate illustration of what happens to a man when he is robbed of his hair. Of course, many things compensate for the lack of inner fulfillment, integrity, and authentic self-empowerment in a man's life, including his propensity to be driven towards material excesses and to wage war.

Perhaps we men are really afraid of ourselves. Perhaps we've been taught and conditioned by the world to fear some deep and profound aspects of our inner selves. Perhaps, the lack of any length, as well as any style in our hair conveys our unconscious need to control whatever terrifyingly powerful reality is symbolized by a full head of hair:

Hair=animal=instinct=sex=woman=feeling=vulnerability=death?

I will further contend that when we deny our hair, we deny a deeper part of ourselves that is intrinsically connected to the organic nature out of which we evolved—although to say we evolved "out of" nature is to deny that in reality *we are the human expression of nature itself.*

Modern man's preoccupation with cropping his hair so close to his head, denying his hair its full and free manifestation, is akin to his preoccupation with controlling and curtailing the earth itself, with chopping down trees, destroying wildlife, decimating indigenous tribes, and oppressing women. Man's fear of the free earth and his impulse to contain, control, and contort it lead to his repression of many things, but ultimately to the repression of his own true nature, all of which is exemplified in the obsessive and mindless cutting off of his hair

VII

LIFE IN THE BOX

THERE HAS RECENTLY been a surge in TV shows—such as *Man VS Wild, Survivor,* and *Season's Deadliest Catch*—featuring man's struggle to survive in outdoor raw elements and unbridled wilderness settings. Evidently our tame and sterile office lives leave us thirsty for nature adventures which are now harder to come by. Does this not demonstrate that, while we can in many ways transcend our native natural environment, *we cannot transcend our instincts* to be involved and engaged in living dramas with that native environment from which we were originally born? Though we imagine and increasingly interact with many new, fantastic modes of man-created reality that are virtually devoid of nature, we may never be able to completely deny the native, "nature beings" that we are—or our need to feel, touch, and smell, to play in rivers and oceans, to climb trees and mountains, and otherwise adventure through woods, prairies, and the varied landscapes of this terrestrial planet.

In the biological sense, we are completely dependent upon this natural earth: the air and water, the dirt and sunlight, the animals, plants, trees, rocks and rivers—everything that sustains us and inspires us to live. Even so, the bulk of our lives is spent "indoors," in enclosed boxes, safe and separate from the wild world of nature—except our nice view through the window. What does this state of affairs do to our spirits, our instincts, and our personalities?

For a people that lives the majority of its life in boxes—our homes, offices, bars, and cars—and much of its cognitive or psychic life through another box, the television/computer, how can we really understand the planet, its needs, its state of balance or imbalance, health or sickness? Simply watching *Man VS Wild* on television—or gaining any other form of *information* about the planet—will never substitute for *the real experience* of nature.

The paradox of the television is that while it exposes us to a great many new ideas, images, and sources of information, it simultaneously isolates us from the world by capturing us within the enclosed dwellings in which we must remain to view it. The television offers audio-visual, cognitive, and conceptual entertainment for many of us. It is a strictly human mode of communication that seems to have replaced the communal fire around which humans of times past gathered to share stories, reflect upon their lives, drum, dance, unfold mythologies, and otherwise experience themselves as a community of people interrelated with the earth.

Nowadays the television—like the computer—is just another pivotal tool used by big industry to divorce humans living in modern societies from our biological, planetary, communal, and ancestral roots. It gives us something to do in our chronic state of displacement and isolation from one another. As Daniel Pinchbeck so eloquently stated:

> Electronic culture created soulless replacement for connective rituals—television supplanted tribal lessons told around the fire; "fast food" consumed in distraction took the place of a shared meal. We substituted matter for Ma-

ter, money for mother's milk, objects for emotional bonds.

Unfortunately, the television has become another of the false gods, the venerated objects with which modern society has entranced and pacified us. Through a hocus-pocus, sleight of hand, everything valued in our lives has been virtually transmuted to a box, as it seems we now live in a sort of looking glass nightmare wherein we see ourselves trapped behind the screen, but can never quite free ourselves from technology's insidious hold upon us.

The more abstract *sense of community* that we acquire from the television is gotten in a detached, third party fashion. Obviously, none of the characters and personas we see on the television will ever know us personally, though we regard them as if they did as we watch them interacting in fictional scenarios that have been imagined by those who write the scripts and screenplays for sitcoms, movies, reality shows, documentaries, and news programs. Yes, I do include news programs as another form of fictionalized entertainment, mainly because select people behind the scenes (often the wealthy) control, manipulate, and contort the information we are given.

Furthermore, even when something sounds believable, as news reports often do, it doesn't mean that it's true. Look at all the misinformation and lies we were fed via TV and media as reasons to invade Iraq; things then considered true—because the government wouldn't lie to us would they?!?—which now have been proven to be false, to have been a plot of deception intended to gather support for the war. Of course it is nearly impossible for any news station to report only the objective truth, as they, like the rest of us, have their own agendas and alliances. The news is obviously crafted as another form of entertainment, as evidenced by their highlights, an emphasis on the day's most alluring crime or scandal, dramas which I suppose have been proven to increase ratings.

But, forgive me ... I digress.

By worshipping television we trade, to the degree of our *attendance*, the experience of an actual living community in which we are profoundly involved for an objective viewing of fictional communities in which we are only objectively and distantly involved as spectators, not participants. Interestingly enough, we tend to view our spectator-involvement with television shows and characters as a kind of pseudo-community which we discuss with each other during the course of our actual day-to-day lives.

In viewing television shows we hold the expectation of being entertained, of being stimulated, made to laugh or cry, or perhaps opened up in the heart or expanded in the mind. Some of us simply want some form of company; we live alone or happen to be alone, or are feeling lonely or bored at the moment, and we'd rather have some form of *human companionship* around us— which, in the case of the television, is really a reminder of the human society in which we live. Of course, utilizing the television as company or companionship is moreover a form of distraction, indicative of *the lack of community* or companionship in our modern society which tends to focus so exclusively on the individual.

On the one hand, the television is a very safe and reliable mode of entertainment; on the other, it is not nearly as meaningful or affecting as the companionship of real, actual people who in fact respond to us as we interact with them.

Sometimes it may prove to be personally helpful to turn off the television—as well as the computer and other technological stimulation devices—in order to frustrate your impulses for immediate gratification, to suspend the perpetual stimulation of your "information receptors," and to experience your anxiety, loneliness, and boredom directly.

Sometimes it's necessary to remain *in the dark,* or to be in silence for just a moment or two, so that your own inner truth can come forth. In the monastic or spiritual retreat model, the individual removes himself or herself from the ever-looming world of external stimulations, taking both ample time and space to reflect upon the inner conditions of his or her life. In this day and age, in which we are constantly over-stimulated, taking time for periods of non-stimulation may serve as a necessary elixir for the frenzied state of our lives, and a prerequisite to reconnect with our *being* which is uniquely *human.*

As a replacement for true community and selfhood, television is another example of the degradation and mortification of humanity that has ensued through our developments in technology.

As our technology progresses, the replacements for true community and selfhood are expanding and rapidly multiplying beyond just the television. Many of these technologies are fun and interesting; the tragedy is that they are largely replacing true human community and awareness of the inner and interpersonal self. On the grand scale, it may be that as a human community and species we no longer know who we are.

PART OF THE SAD REALITY of modern life is that many of us do live alone or we live far from our families—or have none—and feel an overwhelming sense of alienation living in "communities," in towns and cities where we do not know or interact with most of the other people. In this age of rampant depression and other mental health disorders requiring medication, could the correlation be any clearer between living in isolation and both mental and moral breakdown in the modern day psyche?

In the middle of the last century, during the *Leave It to Beaver* generation of the 1940s and 1950s, American culture was depicted as occurring within the context of the nuclear family. The reality of that depiction has unraveled as the focus on the individual continues to take precedence and the divorce rate, as well as the percentage of unmarried adults, increases.

The mythos of the nuclear family has lost popularity as we question the value and purpose of marriage and family. Meanwhile, fundamental shifts in our society have propelled us away from domestic and traditional family-oriented lifestyles into more urban, technology-driven, and individual-oriented lifestyles.

As the most cherished, inherited foundations and structures of our society undergo a radical metamorphosis, the positive side is that we discover new ways of being and expressing ourselves, but the negative side is that we often risk losing our sense of self in a society of strangers.

THE TELEVISION, HOWEVER, appears to have had a lasting appeal throughout the successive decades of our cultural transformations—it's been seventy-five years since the first television came on the scene in 1946—and, in this sense, has been our *constant companion* for quite some time. The medium of the television can be viewed as an artful mode of imaginative expression and as a miraculous source of entertainment and information. The depiction of life and reality via the television is, indeed, a sort of wonderland—just imagine how a person living 10,000 years ago would respond to a television! However, the manner in which many of us have virtually integrated the television into our daily lifestyles has become a form of addiction in which we lose our will to live our lives creatively, or to go out and engage the world directly.

Another negative aspect of the television is that it focuses exclusively on our visual and auditory capacities while neglecting our other senses, promoting an atrophy of the body as we sit around lazily watching it. It displays life, human relationships, and nature as things that can be contained in a box—while they obviously cannot—and thereby threatens the integrity of our collective experiential framework through diminishing the potential of our human condition with *representations* of life which are not truly life, yet are presented as, and in our experience are beginning to replace, life itself.

The television *represents* reality, but we rely upon it as if it were *a direct experience of* reality, which it is not. Of course, we do this because from the time we are born the television is presented to us as a normal mode of experiencing life and reality— and yet, in truth, it is at least one gigantic step removed from direct experience.

Over the years of our modern technological developments the options of viewing television have expanded, have indeed multiplied exponentially. When I was a small child living in rural Vermont, we received about three channels—which we often times had to work to bring into focus by adjusting metal antennae that rested directly on top of the TV itself. Back then, not all televisions were in color, and watching programs in black & white was a completely viable and acceptable option. One does not miss that which has not yet been invented, so having three channels to choose from was normal and satisfying.

When I became a teenager, the channel options expanded to about thirteen or so—an impressive leap from our previous number of options. Also, the VCR was invented, so we began to rent and view movies at home—another grand expansion in our television pleasure viewing options! This was the new breakthrough technology, and at that time—the early 80s—it was very exciting.

In my early adulthood, living on my own and with roommates, I curtailed my television viewing for some time and did not own a television for many years. At large, however, cable television became available, and these days, depending on how much you want to spend, there are options of viewing hundreds of channels of a vast variety of programs. Our development of television programming has been ongoing and significant, and will likely continue far into the future.

I wonder why the television is so important to our society, this obsessive, never-ending development of what began as a small box with a black and white screen that often crackled in and out of focus.

Why do we have such an insatiable need for information and entertainment? To what end are we constantly making bigger and better electronic contraptions with which to astound ourselves?

And why are we so mercilessly enamored with these things? Is it merely our fondness for developing technology? For inventing increasingly elaborate machines which can *service* us?

Why do we need to be continually "wowed" by technology?

Are we simply an endlessly emotionally ravenous culture, inherently unfulfilled and forever reaching for the next best thing that we imagine will give us some inner alignment with the universe that might finally make us feel truly *turned on*?

In recent years, as our technology has developed, the quality of the television has also improved as flat screen, wide screen, and profoundly enlarged screen televisions have come into vogue. We now have television-based audio-visual set-ups—which we refer to as "home theatre systems" (a label that surely strokes our entitled egos)—that cost as much as $75,000. These systems fuse together top quality stereo equipment with advanced television technologies. In the arena of entertainment, we live in a society that wants it all and strives to get it, to continually out-do, outperform, and upgrade its existing modes of entertainment via television, computer, internet, cellular phone, iPod, and virtual-cyber technologies.

And through all these modes of entertainment, notwithstanding their excessive potential for delivering incredible forms of sensational stimulation, the body remains inert, sacrificed like a tragic victim of mute societal madness.

Our focus on the television and other technological forms of entertainment is indeed religious, as we worship their very existence. In *the new and enlightened world*, our fervor with technological devices is a compensation for having lost our spiritual connection with the earth, with ourselves, and with one another. Our technological inventions all too often distract us from our lack of genuine fulfillment, and our lack of creative and compassionate, interconnected human and planetary community.

Our fascination with gadgets covers over a profound absence of inner emotional and psychological fulfillment with ourselves and our lives, a profound emptiness in our hearts, and a profound disconnect and alienation of our souls from the earth and cosmos.

In this age of utterly frenzied addiction to modern man-made marvels of technology it is becoming increasingly difficult for us to even discern the existence of our souls or to recognize the reality of soul in the world. Even mentioning the word soul is an inherent affront to many of us with our thoroughly urban and technology-saturated lives.

How can soul, nature, and our own *soul nature* continue to exist in an instantaneous electronic world of cyber technology?

And how do humans relate to their souls once they are both entranced and enslaved by machines?

Mechanically.

Thus, we have undergone the mechanization not only of our bodies and our souls, but, tragically, the mechanization of the entire ecology and biosphere in which we live.

AS A CULTURE AND TECHNOLOGICAL SOCIETY, if we continue to move forward without ever stopping to look back towards wherefrom we came, how can we ever exercise our capacity to consider or reflect upon who, or what, we are becoming? It seems we've lost perspective and balance in our lives as we're forever falling full-throttle into the future. Because of our monovision, fixated forward upon the fantasized future, nothing is relative to anything else anymore. There is just this continual pounding of an absolute mad certainty upon the path of progress.

We've externalized our souls, aborted our spirits, and filled in the empty spaces with the detritus of a chaotic collective unconscious.

Could it be that we've trapped ourselves inside our own constricting conceptual constructs, manifested as the box of television, and the circus show of technology that has entrained us into an incessant need for external stimulation?

Television sedates the masses by providing a perpetual mode of mental masturbation. But it does not provide a true or satisfying replacement for a meaningful experience of our living humanity.

Because nothing can.

Perhaps the imagined apocalypse that is gradually building in our collective psyche is symbolic of our need to free ourselves from ourselves—in breaking through, we must break ourselves open and break out of our *pre-programmed* societal paradigm. Because the dream we're dreaming is quickly becoming a nightmare. Our fascination with the television and other forms of man-made technological materialism only confirms this.

We need to turn off the *tele-vision* of technology and wake up to find a more expansive *human-vision* of life that answers the deeper longings of our souls, as well as the needful dreams of the planetary being upon which we live.

VIII

EVOLUTION OF THE SPIRIT

THOUGH MOST OF US TAKE for granted the assumption that humanity has indeed *evolved* over the millennia into our own current version of modern Western technological society, we should stop to examine these assumptions. I suppose even *evolution* is a concept whose definition should be examined. Our idea of evolution, *to evolve*, is that of the tadpole growing legs and climbing ashore and the monkey descending from the tree, shedding hair, and metamorphosing into a flesh covered and more astutely intelligent human species. Our idea is that evolution is a natural, almost God-granted or divinely planned progression of life from beginning, basic, and limited forms into increasingly advanced, complex, and unlimited forms.

So we speak of the evolution of fish into lizards, or—in terms of humanity—of a culture that carries water in jugs on their heads a mile to the village into a culture that merely turns a knob to procure running water. However, we must ask ourselves if our vision of human evolution is not self-serving and limited in scope to our own unique modern cultural values.

From the tribal person's point of view, perhaps carrying water from its source to the place of human habitation is an enjoyable activity that is part of a daily connection and relationship with other members of the community and the natural world. Perhaps carrying water is also a grounding experience, enabling time for reflection and contemplation. For the tribal person, the gathering of water could make ordinary life more like a ritual; it could make the relationship with water more of a mindful and sacred experience.

Perhaps actually seeing where the water comes from, a river or a lake, grants a greater appreciation of the water in a larger environmental and spiritual context. I imagine that witnessing other animals coming to the lake or river to drink and bathe engenders an enhanced sense of place and participation in earthly life. And perhaps spending so much time and energy to gather a single jug of water conveys a deeper appreciation of the miracle of water and all the benefits of cleansing, refreshment, and sustenance that it provides.

In our modern *evolved* world we have much less appreciation for the water we use because it comes to us so easily; therefore, we truly lack any kind of significant or conscious relationship with water. We've become entitled with the daily expectation of limitless supplies of water at any temperature we desire. We use much more water than we need, and we waste more water than we should. Also, our water is bleached and bitter to the tongue because, unlike the tribal person's water, it has become polluted by our own industries—although, over the years, modern industry has also poisoned indigenous people's water sources throughout the entire world. Because many of us must now purchase our drinking water, perhaps the monetary value we now place upon water will enable us to realize its importance and will lead to needed changes in our industries which pollute the water.

Reflecting upon the two drastically divergent attitudes towards water, the question arises, "Which culture has the more *evolved* relationship with water?" The Western world has made its values very clear: efficiency, comfort, and ease. However, in gaining the valued conditions we desire, we have also lost the earthly qualities of living that make us feel more alive, connected, and involved in the natural processes of life. Indeed, our entire way of life has shifted from focus upon nature to a focus upon mechanical man-made processes involving a mélange of industrial and technological forces.

Both the modern and the ancient ways of relationship with water are valid. However, when we judge other cultural ways of living as inferior to ours through concepts such as "evolution," and through labeling pre-Western societies as "primitive," we lose respect for these societies—as well as the valuable paradigms of living that they embrace—and act in ways that assume we have the right to change them as we please. I believe such practices are inhumane and unethical because they have been infinitely harmful to non-Western cultures.

Why is it so difficult for modern Westerners to allow non-Westerners who are not interested in our way of life to retain their own?

Why are we so bent on converting others to our own ways, if not for the very wrong reason of profiting from their resources?

We must develop tolerance and respect for ways of being that are different from our own and which we may not understand or even want to understand. In this age of expanding global awareness it is more important than ever for all human cultures to coexist peacefully upon the planet.

To pre-Western people the earth was viewed as a sacred, fertile, and creative force. According to the modern Western scientific perspective, the ocean is merely a body of water filled with cold-blooded creatures; therefore, we don't feel quite so bad or guilty about poisoning it through oil spills, massive amounts of garbage, and daily run-off of toxic substances. Similarly, we are able to clear-cut entire mountains and valleys, wiping out enormous panoramas of trees, flora and fauna, and existing ecosystems with no regard for the animal inhabitants whose lives are devastated and destroyed as well.

We see the trees as resources for our lumber companies, to funnel into the building of tract homes and Taco Bell eateries. The land we clear becomes our own *fertile ground* for roads, strips malls, and man-made conglomerations of industry and habitation, for a human culture based in separation from, and subjugation of, nature. However, our use of the word "clear" in this context is utterly deceptive as it truly denotes the desecration and demolishing of the land.

In our current mode of society we choose to live against the earth, in spite of the earth, at odds with the earth, and in domination over the earth.

But why should the rest of the world be forced to live like this?

Our form of civilization is based on the transmutation of nature into our own man-made societal forms which obliterate the original balance and well-being of nature. And our reigning religion, Christianity, more or less justifies this attitude with its assertion that only man can know God, that only man can be "delivered from sin," and that only man can be resurrected in the next eternal life called Heaven.

I guess there are no animals or plants or trees or rivers in Heaven, unless they are transported there by God just for looks.

This aspect of exclusion which Christianity perpetrates upon the world—upon all the other species in the whole of nature, as well as all other non-Christian human beings—is ridiculous, wrong, and murderously harmful to the earth and our relationship with it.

Because pre-Western cultures—such as the Native Americans who not so long ago freely roamed and lived upon the land we now occupy—viewed God the Creator as living in and through Creation, and as being inextricably connected with nature, they respected the earth and strove to live in an interdependent harmony with it, not as an independent ruler in domination over nature, as do we.

In his book *Columbus and other Cannibals,* Jack D. Forbes writes, "The life of Native American peoples revolved around the concept of the sacredness, beauty, power and relatedness of *all forms* of existence."

Hence, in the view of Native American peoples, the ocean is considered to be a sacred, living being with a presence and a spirit. To pollute Her would be the same as pouring poison down your mother's throat. Native Americans did not wantonly chop down trees, clear away the land, and otherwise demolish nature and the living environment of animals. Rather, they revered trees, plants, and animals, and prayed to their spirits upon taking their lives.

Demonstrating the interconnected way in which Native Americans lived with the earth, Forbes writes:

> When a plant, tree or animal is to be killed, first, the need must be great; second, permission is asked for, if time allows; third, the creature is thanked; and fourth, dances, prayers and ceremonies are used to further thank the creatures so killed and to help those that are alive to grow and prosper.

Indigenous, pre-Western people did not pretend to own the world as do we and, in fact, viewed this perspective as a very ignorant and destructive form of insanity. From the looks of the world created by modern society, it appears that they were right.

The following is an abbreviated version of a famous and well-known speech given in 1851 by Chief Seattle of the Suquamish tribe as part of the Native American response to the United States government's "offer" to purchase two million acres of land for $150,000:

> How can you buy or sell the sky, the warmth of the land? The idea is strange to us. If we do not own the freshness of the air and the sparkle of the water, how can you buy them? Every part of this earth is sacred to my people. Every shining pine needle, every sandy shore, every mist in the dark woods, every clearing and humming insect is holy in the memory and experience of my people. The sap which courses through the trees carries the memories of the red man. We are part of the earth and it is part of us ... We know that the white man does not understand our ways. One portion of land is the same to him as the next, for he is a stranger who comes in the night and takes from the land whatever he needs. The earth is not his brother, but his enemy, and when he has conquered it, he moves on ... He treats his mother, the earth, and his brother, the sky, as things to be bought, plundered, sold like sheep or bright beads ... Whatever befalls the earth befalls the sons of the earth ... This we know: the earth does not belong to man; man belongs to the earth. All things are connected.

This speech is an amazingly beautiful and poetic prophecy. Although, perhaps, it idealizes and romanticizes native life, it also rings clear with essential truth. This speech epitomizes the reality that Native American spirituality is significantly connected to everyday life and interactions with the planet, not separated out into a special Sunday event as in our modern world.

Many pre-Western religions or spiritualities are referred to as forms of animism, a mode of religious thought which basically connotes that God—*the Creating Spirit of Life*—lives in the world. Hence, all things in the God-created natural world are seen to be alive with the spark of the Creator, the divine energy that created the world. When the world of nature is viewed as an expression, or an extension of the Creator, one maintains a sense of reverence, respect, and awe for all things. In our modern world of "Man the Creator," we tend to mock such spiritual views as naïve and dumb, yet perhaps our denial and refutation of the life-force animating the world of nature is part of our own chronic sense of alienation.

While the Western paradigm frowns upon *animism* as a religion or spirituality, conversely, it is glorified in our *animated* movies and cartoons, wherein plants and animals are imagined and depicted as having human-like personalities. On the one hand, through mimicry, this trend robs plants and animals of their own unique identity and dignity, while on the other, it seems to be at least a sign that we moderns acknowledge, if only through our fantasy-play, that the world of animals and plants is indeed alive with volition and concerns very similar to those of humankind.

In this respect, at least, perhaps our culture is more interested in animism as a potential worldview than we consciously recognize.

RETURNING TO THE CONSIDERATION of evolution and the question of whether or not we have indeed evolved or progressed intelligently from the "primitive world" to "technological life," I would have to say that, although we have made many interesting and useful developments—consider the toaster oven and the pogo stick!—in many ways we have created undue suffering and mayhem that does not indicate an intelligent progression or evolution of life.

The amount of death and mortifyingly horrendous infliction we have enacted upon the world of man through our invention of firearms and weapons is so monumental that it can hardly be summed up. When the technology we develop to advance ourselves is also used in the service of destroying other people, cultures, species, and the planet itself, one must question our "process of evolution."

Do we—as a modern and technologically advanced society—consider ourselves to be evolving through our perpetration of pain and destruction upon the remainder of the globe? We now hold the technological power through nuclear weapons to obliterate the entire human species; but if we vanished from this planet, in all probability non-human life would continue, and perhaps the entire cycle of *evolution* as we know it would begin all over again.

By defining evolution as a "survival of the fittest," some might uphold our modern theory of evolution as 100% authentic and valid. This perspective would justify our deleterious impact on other cultures, species, and life-forms upon the earth, explicating that we are naturally ingrained with an *evolutionary instinct* to progress, to forward ourselves at all costs, thereby ensuring our own survival.

From this perspective, the more powerful, safe, and secure we are, the greater are our options for getting what we want in the world. However, *to be human also means to have a heart*, a huge capacity for compassion and justice in our interactions with the world of others. And yet, humans seem to be the only species on the planet that possess the trait of killing each other with such enormous magnitude and frequency—a trait that appears to be more than just our capacity for advanced methods of infliction.

With the other species, *the big fish eats the small fish*, but only as needed, and not ALL the small fish, otherwise what would the big fish eat tomorrow?

Perhaps we "enlightened" human beings of the modern world need to redefine our concept of evolution, otherwise our view remains that of one species or culture—namely ours—advancing at the expense of other species or cultures. Perhaps we could come to understand evolution not only on a biological or cultural basis, but also as a spiritual reality: evolution as a conscious, co-creative, and inclusive process of adaptation and flourishing in which all involved are considered and benefitted.

Most religious figures, the more *evolved* personages of humankind who are deeply admired and emulated—such as Jesus Christ, Buddha, Krishna, and Muhammad—taught love, compassion and peace as paramount features of a living relationship with God, and crucial to our human spiritual development. Obviously these teachings indicate living in ways that promote harmony, not conflict, with other people, and peaceful, not devastating, actions upon the earth.

We are coming to the collective awareness that when we hurt others we also hurt ourselves, and that when we harm the earth we also harm humanity. So, if we want to exercise our superior intelligence, perhaps we should increasingly act on that awareness by seeking to help the world—instead of simply inflating our own ideas and ego-powered agendas through the globalization of democracy and capitalism—by creating peace and an augmentation of the world's well-being.

We need to realize that other cultures live according to their own values, not ours.

Therefore, what right do we have to impinge our own will upon them?

True evolution—the evolution of the spirit—is not just about advancing our own concerns, but also understanding the concerns of others and acting in ways that respect those concerns.

IX

RETURN TO THE TRIBAL

THE TERM "TRIBAL" has become fashionable these days, as has our interest in tribal culture—however superficial it may be. This is evidenced by the enthrallment the American public has with TV shows such as *Survivor*. It is ironic that we have constructed a technologically advanced society, virtually safe from the threat of beast and vermin; yet at night, when the day's work is done, millions gather around their TVs to watch shows like *Survivor,* in which citizens of the modern world—people just like us—are temporarily immersed into "primitive" and natural wilderness environments in an entertaining experiment designed to determine how well they will cope, adapt, or otherwise survive in a sort of makeshift tribal-group situation.

Although we experience this interest from the safety and comfort of our couches and easy chairs, and through the objective and removed medium of a television, we have evidently not progressed far beyond our fascination with indigenous cultures and the ways they live in close proximity with the earth. If we imagine the trend of *technological humanity* into the future, we can hypothesize that one day soon science will develop a readily available suit that one can don which will enable a virtual-reality experience of the *Survivor* TV show, or any other known or imagined environmental simulation, so that one will never have to physically leave the comfort and familiarity of one's home.

Survivor was one of the first "reality" TV shows granting citizens of the modern world, who tend to work in factories and office buildings all day, a glimpse into what life would be like lived in a primordial nature environment, in the context of a small *tribal-like* culture. Although the popularity of this television program probably only demonstrates a casual interest in tribal cultures, in the past couple of decades we of the modern Western world have expressed our interest in tribal cultures in many other, more deeply genuine and compelling ways.

One of these ways is through a profusion of published writings on indigenous cultures and spirituality, as well as on shamanism—the original way of healing body and soul—by authors as classic and well known as Carlos Castaneda, and as recent and avant-garde as Daniel Pinchbeck. The interest in tribal culture can also been seen in the rising practice by modern Westerners of Native American rituals, such as the Inipi ceremony—more commonly known as the sweat lodge—, the vision quest, and the Sun Dance ritual.

There was also the rise, in the late 1980s, of the mythopoetic men's movement, led by charismatic figures such as Robert Bly, Michael Meade, and James Hillman, in which many of the ancient ideas and practices of both Western and non-Western cultural traditions—blending together modern psychological thought and a poetic appreciation of consciousness—are explored in experiential healing gatherings. Women have also explored these dimensions of consciousness in gender specific gatherings as well, as made amply apparent by the rise and popularity of feminism.

There are many community-based endeavors that are not gender specific, in which tribal ways are explored as avenues of personal and collective growth for the modern person. Some of these gatherings are less directive, though highly creative events in which one's degree of participation is completely voluntary, such as the annual Burning Man festival and ongoing Rainbow Gatherings that occur around the world. These carnivalesque events incorporate highly experimental ways of being, thinking, and interrelating in a creative community setting, in which various forms of artful spirituality—such as altar making, prayer and chanting circles, processions, parades, meditations and innovative rituals—are explored.

There are also a varied assortment of music festivals in which one may encounter elements of tribal life, such as camping out in a natural setting, all night drum circles, music and dancing, and the application of various mind-altering substances that expand the modern mind into more open-ended and transpersonal dimensions.

Traditionally tribal practices, such as West African, Middle Eastern, and Latin drumming and dance, have also recently become popular forms of study, expression, and entertainment. Other tribal realities of interest to Westerners include firedancing, communal healing circles, Tantra—an Eastern practice of sacred sexuality—massage, Reiki, Tarot and I-Ching divination, experiential shamanism, and the rise of ecotourism in which modern Westerners visit indigenous or quasi-indigenous cultures to experience aspects of original tribal ritual and ceremony. All these factors indicate that, although we live in a culture obsessed with the material advancements of the individual, we reveal our longings for the dynamic attributes of indigenous, tribal life in many ways.

From the mainstream appeal of experimental television programs involving aspects of tribal culture, to the more sincere seekers of an authentic awakening to ancient realities, our modern, technological culture is striving to remain connected with our roots as a human species. While our global population sky-rockets and we spend more time in the impersonal company of strangers, it's reassuring to know there are atmospheres of endeavor in which modern folks come together to explore an earth-based, creative, or ritual experience of human community involving spiritual values and not simply profane consumerism. Once again, we see that *the way forward* is not a straight, linear line of uncompromising technological advancements, but a weaving or spiraling back and forth through the rich, inner, and historical dimensions of our human heritage, in which to evolve we must integrate our past with our future in a creative communion which makes sense for the present moment.

Machines and technology are amazing inventions of modern Western society that remain meaningless without a vision of human life and community that works for all of us and which affirms and celebrates all aspects of our collective human capacity. The modern world offers sleek versions of material reality that emphasize a *transcendence of the soil* into elevated sensational and conceptual dimensions that become overly-sanitized and despotic without the balanced grounding of a bodily connection with the earth.

Unfortunately, elevated material reality—or a materialistic relationship to life—also results in an abdication of the soul, which represents our true inner nature. Once this is accomplished, the scene is set for an ongoing psychological crisis.

Although most of us live in cities, surrounded by concrete, cars, and man-made sprawl, our *return to the tribal* demonstrates our human need to remain spiritually intact, terrestrially identified, experiential seekers of life. Tribal consciousness is a field afar from the individualizing, separatist consciousness of modern capitalist society. In the depths of our souls we retain a need to feel our underlying interconnection and unity with all of humanity and the planet from which we sprang. Modern life is like the icing on a many-layered cake—it covers what is beneath it, but in no way can it ever completely hide or abolish those deeper layers upon which it was built.

The problem with modern technological life is that it proceeds ahead blindly as if it could ignore the past. It soars everupwards, as if the downward or inward directions—symbolic of significant psycho-spiritual realities—did not exist. But our pull to tribal dimensions of consciousness reveal these other directions in which reality points—in seeming opposition to our current everyday reality—as highly significant and essential to our spiritual well-being.

In the deeper reckoning of our fascination with tribal culture perhaps we are simply identifying with our greater planetary sense of being and molecular history which is embedded in the earth and universe as a cosmic reality.

X

THE SPIRITUAL REALITY
OF NATURE

"When you finally understood that nature was the
imagination of the Gods, you realized that your nature
hunted your own soul inside this enormous imagination."
~Martin Prechtel, *Secrets of the Talking Jaguar*

THE UNFORTUNATE FACT that modern society is primarily devoted to money and material things, as opposed to human beings and spiritual things, is affirmed by an attribute of our culture that the great mythologist Joseph Campbell remarked upon in an interview with Bill Moyers, which was transcribed into the book *The Power of Myth*. During the interview, while discussing the topic of sacred sites and places, Campbell remarked:

You can tell what's informing a society by what the tallest building is. When you approach a medieval town, the cathedral is the tallest thing in the place. When you approach an eighteenth-century town, it is the political palace that is the tallest thing in the place And when you approach a modern city, the tallest places are the office buildings, the centers of economic life.

It is fairly straightforward symbolic thinking to conclude that the tallest structure built by any society represents their highest, most lofty ambitions. The shift from cathedral to political palace to office building or bank denotes the new direction our culture has taken in worshiping money and materialism over that of God or even our relationships with one another. Campbell states, "The goal of early life was to live in constant consciousness of the spiritual principle." However, in modern times we have little room for the spiritual as our lives are centered around obsessive concerns with material reality and money.

Over the past couple of centuries our primary focus has quickly shifted from God and the divine—transpersonal matters concerning our spiritual life, mission, and post-mortem fate—to almost entirely selfish matters regarding how well we can fare in this transitory material realm.

This shift in perspective, perception, and consciousness has narrowed and intensified our area of awareness to our own personal self-invested ego interests. Having become largely liberated from the expectations that God, religion, or spiritual mores and obligations have upon us, we think and act less and less with regard to others or how our actions will affect other beings, including the planet.

With a more potent focus on our own self-serving concerns, unencumbered by what God or family or our social group thinks we should do, we've discovered more of our individual potential and become able to achieve greater heights of personal success.

However, while we've benefited in many ways from this shift in attention, we've also become increasingly self-centered, a trend which has led to a cultural crisis in the area of our relationships. Meanwhile, our sense of belonging to our communities, our culture, and connection with spirituality have waned as well. Consequently, we've lost some of the richness and depth of our *humanness.*

Without meaningful roots our relationships topple over easily. Because we value our expanded individual freedoms so immensely, we often lack the deep bonds of commitment to something or someone other than ourselves. Look at the modern propensity of fathers to leave their families and sever communication with their children. Without a transpersonal, or even cultural sense of identity, of being part of something greater than one's own personal self-interests or ego, we invariably experience existential crisis.

We've been beguiled by the allure of wealth and power as equating with true inner happiness. But who we are cannot ultimately be satisfied or fulfilled by our bank accounts and our personal accumulation of material things. Nonetheless, this mirage has been instilled into our consensual reality as a centerpiece of the grand American Illusion that divides us against ourselves and from one another.

Contrary to our modern fascination with materiality, we all have an intrinsic spiritual aspect which impels us to celebrate the beautiful mystery of our lives and our ultimate unity with the world—as evidenced by certain "holy days," as well as our own internal longings for ecstatic fulfillment. Material things may compel us, but they inevitably grow old and break down.

Ancient peoples realized more profoundly than we do that when you die you can't take your material possessions with you— you can't take your car, or your clothing, or your computer; you can't take your house or all the wonderful things you have accumulated; you can't even take your family, your friends, or your own body. All you can take with you is, perhaps, your soul ...

Most religions teach us to *believe* in God; but how are we to *experience* God, to actually perceive and feel the presence of

God? Indeed, what is God—beyond an image or a concept in our minds—if we cannot feel, sense, or encounter God in an experiential way? The direct experience of spiritual reality in Western culture seems like some far-off, intangible concept which is difficult to attain, especially reserved for those few individuals who claim to have had encounters with the divine, with alternate dimensions or metaphysical beings such as angels, ghosts, or extraterrestrials.

For many people the concept of "spirit," let alone the experience, is both abstract and obtuse—it doesn't seem to have much context in our overly rational, scientific, and technology-based world. What does it mean when we say something has a spirit? According to many ancient traditions having a "spirit" simply means that something is alive, that it has a life-force. Along these modes of perception, an animal such as a dog, cat, or badger obviously has a spirit, it is alive and expresses its life-force in many ways. In this sense, a green clover plant also has a spirit; it is alive, it responds to the sun, it grows, then dies, and when eaten transfers its life-force to an animal or human who utilizes its energy to live.

A definite distinction can be made between an animal or a plant and something like a plastic chair or a metal trash can. The plastic chair was made by man and does not appear to have much of a spirit; it is not alive in the biological or spiritual sense. Therefore, a plastic chair is not a spiritual, but a material thing.

Living things of nature, which were made by a force greater than human beings and are an intrinsic part of biological, cosmic reality, all have a spirit because they are alive and actively interacting with a greater, whole, living environment. Thus considered, all things in the natural world have a spirit and are basically spiritual because they have an in-born life-force. The world of modern, man-made things, on the other hand, generally lack spirit, are not living, and are not essential to the greater order and harmony of life—although we may consider them essential to our own. Therefore, most man-made things would be considered material, not spiritual.

There are exceptions to this "rule"—the experience of spirit is not dictated by some absolute objective determination, but is also a subjective and idiosyncratic matter—as humans are also an interactive, interrelated part of nature. We create things out of wood, stone, and other natural materials that are, in a sense, still very much alive and radiant with the spirit of nature. We also interact with nature to co-create spectacles of beauty, such as gardens, ponds, or parks that are still very much alive in the biological, thus spiritual, sense.

There is also the realm of art in which we fashion sensuous or aesthetic objects of beauty through our creative imaginations which appear to have a different kind of spirit or life-force, not necessarily biological or elemental, but which indeed carries the capacity to *move* the spirit inside us.

The spirit is not something beyond this earth and sky, but the essence of that which animates the entire planet—inclusive of all its living beings—and perhaps the cosmos as well.

The spirit of life can be seen in the way a bird flies or in how the wind blows through the trees, in the miracle of sunlight as it illuminates green grass or the sound and smell of ocean waves breaking against the cliffs. The spirit is not just an abstract idea or image of a distant omnipotent being who secretly monitors our every move. Some cultures refer to spirit primarily as the breath—the flow of life—that moves involuntarily in and out of our lungs. Various creation mythologies, including the Bible, depict spirit as the breath with which God breathed life into the world. Without the breath, after all, there could be no life, no animals, no humans. Even plants breathe!

Indigenous cultures recognize the spiritual reality of nature more readily and in greater profundity than do we of the "developed world." As Martin Prechtel came to realize during his initiation into Mayan culture, "The speech of the Gods was nature." In this spiritual paradigm of living, "the things of the world were addressed instead of being discussed." This is because the things of the world were recognized as *beings* infused with spirit and existing in the world interdependently with human beings.

Contra wise, what we have developed in modern society is a way of life through manipulation of nature that separates and insulates us from nature, as well as from the energetic forces and ways of being associated with life in communion with nature. In this, our modern mode of interaction with nature, there is little awe, respect, or genuine contact with dignified and autonomous forces of creation.

Indigenous, pre-Western peoples tend to regard the world of nature as sacred because it grants them life: the air they breathe; the fire of the sun that warms their bodies and provides the vital force that grows the plants they eat; the earth itself that provides food, shelter, and clothing for survival; the water that cleans, refreshes, and sustains them. The elements of earth and universe are sacred in pre-Western paradigms that realize how vital they are to human life, to our enjoyment of living, and our very survival. Recognizing that the human being is a particular extension and manifestation of life on earth, most indigenous cultures interact with nature in ways that express respect for the sanctity of all life.

THE DISCUSSION OF THE SPIRITUAL reality of nature is important because it affects how we live, how we think, and how we relate to the earth. When we surround ourselves with non-spiritual, non-living things, such as an overabundance of concrete, steel, and plastic, we feel less than alive, and we lose touch with the ancient vibrancy and energy of the natural world. This is why office environments and factories, hospitals and schools, and even our homes are often times "dead zones" that leave us feeling depleted and uninspired. When we cut ourselves off from our source, which is nature, we begin to die; we wilt inside like neglected house plants, and we feel frustrated like dogs who are penned up in empty houses all day long.

When we surround ourselves with uninspiring man-made environments our life energy tends to diminish, whereas when we are surrounded by natural environments our life energy tends to increase and to thrive. This is why we often take vacations to tranquil, natural areas by the beach or in the mountains, in remote places far away from the daily hub-bub of city society. There is a reason why nature rejuvenates us, because nature is the surrounding source, or matrix, of energy in which, by which, and out of which we were created to live. Because we live in a man-made world divided from nature, this truth is very hard for citizens of modern society to grasp.

To us, the suburban sprawl of roads, cars, buildings and industry seems more natural than nature itself—because we grew up in it, and because we've adapted ourselves to it.

However, what modern human society has created is a far cry from nature, and its impact upon us is far less nourishing. In truth, *we are the manifestation of nature in human form.* Although we have a more evolved brain and capacity for conscious self-reflection, we are made of basically the same substance as other animals, and with many of the same needs.

In contrast with an experience of nature, the bright fluorescent lights of a sterile office filled with cold plastic objects, metalbound machines, artificial countertops and fake plants seems ridiculous at the least, but truly unfulfilling and somehow wrong at the worst. There is something "anti-life" about such environments that were conjured by capitalists to promote the influx of material profit. They share no harmonic resonance with our bodies or our spirits, and provide a condition of ugliness that makes us feel disjointed and out of place. While offices tend to make us feel claustrophobic, antsy, and irritable, most natural places are welcoming, so we feel more open, energetic, nourished and alive.

Nature has an inherent power, energy, and presence which you can sense and feel. To elicit something of this experience, try this brief guided visualization. As you read along, close your eyes intermittently to fully register the images and scenarios described.

Imagine you are outside in a meadow on a warm, sunny day. The atmosphere is tranquil and inviting, and you hear a bubbling creek running nearby. The insects are humming, and birds sing melodically in the distance as a gentle breeze plays upon your face and arms. Green rolling hills with long wild grasses surround you. Looking more closely you see that the hills are spotted with flowers of various colors and kind. Take a few moments to fully feel the impact this scenario has on your body and your mind. At the edge of the meadow, just before the bubbling creek, stands a large prominent tree that captures your attention. You slowly begin to approach the tree, and with each step you see more clearly the colors of its leaves, the shapes of its branches, and the textures of the bark upon its trunk.

Take a little time to see the tree. Look at it as if this were the first time you every really saw a tree. Notice its intricate characteristics, how it reaches high into the sky above you, its branches and leaves shimmering in the breeze, and how it disappears down beneath your feet into the ground below you through an unseen network of roots that drink in nourishment from the soil. You may even notice animals, such as squirrels or birds who inhabit the tree.

Moving closer to the tree, notice its aroma and the energy it seems to emanate. Moving right up next to the tree, put your hand on its trunk, feeling the distinct sensation of its bark. Feel the immense presence of the tree and all it has lived through for many long years here at the edge of the meadow, next to the creek. Allow yourself to truly *feel* the energy and life-force of the tree. Now take a moment to see what has changed inside you during this visualization. Notice the state of your body, your mind, and your emotions. Take a minute to appreciate how this visualization upon a tree in nature has affected your inner presence and state of being. Then gradually return to a full awareness of your actual present surroundings.

ALTHOUGH THE BASIS OF THE SPIRIT is to be found in nature, this does not refute the existence of metaphysical spiritual reality, of God or the divine, as existing or originating, in non-physical, non-terrestrial dimensions. However, here on earth, one cannot exist without the other. Physical creatures—such as humans, animals, and plants—are beings that have an inherent living, breathing, and vibrational quality which is directly connected to the physical nature source of our energy, life, and consciousness.

But the physical is not only physical, as we have come to believe it is; the physical is also spiritual—they are two sides of the same reality. Although a non-physical, or non-exclusively physical, cosmic creator may exist, on this planet and in this lifetime, we are first and foremost physical beings. Without the body there is no life, no mind, no emotions, no thought, nothing.

As an overly-scrutinizing and thought-identified species, most of what we consider to be spiritual is really a matter of belief, or even preference. It is rare that we base our considerations of what is spiritual on our direct perception or experience. This is because the modern Western paradigm, more so than any other, has made the sharpest distinction and split between mind and body, which has also manifested as a split between nature and spirit—in which we favor the mind and a disembodied or "de-natured" interpretation of spirituality—thus hindering our potential for perceiving the spiritual in the physical, and for perceiving the essence of the Creator in the world of Creation.

This split manifests as a monumental division within us and a fragmentation in our sense of self that leads to much heartache, pain, and conflict. Elaborating upon the work of Jean Gebser, Daniel Pinchbeck, author of *2012: The Return of Quetzalcoatl,* writes, "In the process of modernity, we first became 'denatured,' cut off from our original relatedness to the natural world, and then 'decultured,' amputated from the skills and artifacts we had created in the place of nature." Thus, we have gradually isolated and sequestered ourselves from nature, the epitome of spirit on earth, followed by a desecration of the soul of humanity through the annihilation of meaningful culture which we call modern society.

The magnanimous man-made madness that we have manifested upon the planet has been accomplished by machines that neglect and betray our human bodies, our human nature, our spirituality, and our connection with the natural planet. Most of us live in a town or city that has been extensively paved upon with asphalt and laid with concrete, designed to support our transport via motor vehicles—those huge, heavy hunks of machinery that guarantee us relatively quick travel over large spans of distance.

The towns and cities in which we live are typically designed such that we will need one of these intricately crafted, ingeniously devised, and exceedingly expensive conglomerations of synthetic materials to navigate through the landscape on our way to work, school, the grocery store, or to visit family and friends.

In the modern town, we take for granted that life necessitates some form of motor vehicle transport. Though most of us can afford a car, some of us cannot and have to rely upon a *communal car*—the bus, train, trolley, or taxi—to get us where we're going. Yes, there is the occasional person who gets around on foot or bike, but they are the exception to the rule. However, the basic assumption of the modern township remains the same: one's own body is not an effective, sufficient, or even acceptable mode of transport.

So you see, in the very blueprint of our communities, we nullify one of the primary functions of the human body, that of locomotion, as we force a dependence upon a machine mode of transport that is actually quite costly and, in fact, lethal. Sure, we walk on the sidewalks, but they are made of concrete, harder and denser than even the asphalt roads upon which the car travels, and after a short while the walking begins to wear on our feet, knees, and legs. There are very rarely any good dirt paths upon which one can walk that lead to any practical place to which one may want to travel.

Call me a crazy mystic, or a hippie freak, but when I walk on a dirt path—directly upon the "flesh of the earth"—I experience an energetic exchange between my body and the planet. Walking upon concrete for any length of time is painful, yet not many of us seem to care. We have learned to accept it as another *essential* aspect of modern civilization.

Because of the split between our bodies and minds—in which our "inferior" bodies are regulated like machines by our "superior" minds—we don't seem to *mind* that the very design of our towns, with their all-encompassing roads and sidewalks, are, in essence, quite hostile to our own God-given, biological, and naturally spiritual bodies.

When inside a car, we don't fully relate to the earth and our natural surroundings as we're zooming by concerned about traffic lights, road signs, and other drivers, not to mention our iPods and text messages. While driving a car we certainly don't notice things as intricately or immediately as we do when we're walking because "*through a glass darkly*" our senses are removed from the natural atmosphere as we experience the world secondhand. Our body, in its disengaged state, becomes an auxiliary function as it drives the machine that is ultimately driving it.

Encaged in shiny mobile boxes of constructed synthetic materials which have been ignited by processed fossil fuels, we are like specimens in an experimental laboratory, removed from direct impact with the world. We get impatient when traffic slows or we hit a red light because deep down we don't want to be strapped in a chair, encased in metal, and stuck behind a glass shield watching the world go by—no, we want to be outside moving on our feet, engaged with the world through our bodies, our senses, and our instincts!

So when the inevitable frustration of driving comes on, we turn up the music or light a cigarette. We yell at other drivers or silently curse them under our breath. Many of us become temporarily insane while driving the car; we call this condition "road rage"—a reaction which demonstrates the fact that we don't belong in such a servile situation, bound to machines, encased inside hunks of metal. Despite our recurrent displeasure, our flat-out violent reactions to this state of affairs, we accept cars and the necessity of driving them as "facts of life."

In addition to, and sometimes as a result of, our irritations with driving and our occasional bouts with road rage, many of us are directly injured, deformed, and killed in car collisions and accidents. In the United States alone, there are over six million car accidents resulting in approximately thirty-eight thousand deaths and almost three million injuries every year. This means that, on average, every single day one hundred and four people die in car accidents in our country alone. These are very tragic figures, and one can imagine that global figures are considerably higher.

However, the toll that cars take on human life does not seem to be very effective in prodding our reconsideration of the car as a mainstay of our societal life. Our dependence on cars demonstrates a significant way in which our current society goes against the grain not only of the spiritual reality of nature, but also the spiritual reality of the body.

It must be a terrible thing to be crushed to death in a car and a horrific industrial nightmare to be involved in a profoundly injurious accident. And yet we would all love a nice, brand new, shiny car, one that goes real fast and makes us look good. Some guys use cars to attract women, cars that express a persona of *powerful and sexual masculinity.* The rich and wealthy employ cars as another way of flaunting their power and social status to the world, as a way of *driving their wealth around town* to show others how special they are. They have luxury cars with all the extras: lush leather interiors, tinted windows, sunroofs, stellar sound systems, and incredible engine magnitude.

In our world, the car functions not only as a mechanism for our transport, but also as a way for us to express our personalities, almost *as an extension of our personalities*—like a second body that carries around our first, flesh and bone, body. After a point, the obsession with cars seems rather silly and pretentious; however, cars remain a huge, foundational cornerstone of our capitalistic enterprises. As a status symbol, questioning the car would be a kick to the ego that many of us are just not willing to risk. And as an integral aspect of the multi-billion dollar oil and automobile industries, any cessation in the use of cars would send a huge segment of our economy into a catastrophic avalanche.

Regardless of our cultural, psychological, and financial dependence on cars, our bodies—being the part of our human identity that is probably closest to nature—are betrayed not only by the design of our towns and cities that require the use of cars for our transport, but also through the air and sound pollution that cars discharge which is harmful to our physical health, psychological well-being, and the overall state of nature as well. Air pollution stemming from the use of motor vehicles has done irreparable damage to the ozone layer, which, according to the United States Environmental Protection Agency, has resulted in "less protection from ultraviolet light [and] will, over time, lead to higher skin cancer and cataract rates and crop damage."

Not only that, a recent BBC report stated that the air pollution caused by car exhaust and industrial chimneys significantly increased both lung cancer and heart disease. The report highlighted a scientific study performed in the United States, and published in the Journal of the American Medical Association, which stated that the fine particulates emitted from car exhaust and industrial chimneys "significantly increases the risk of dying from heart disease." A related study in the United Kingdom concluded that "10,000 people a year might be dying as a result of particulate pollution."

The toxicity of the exhaust which issues from the tailpipe on any car is further evidenced by the propensity of those intent on ending their own lives. This deadly capacity of cars is utilized by suicidal folks who simply turn on their car in the enclosed space of a garage and wait, as carbon monoxide fills their lungs, for death to take them away from their worldly woes. Yes, for all the wonderful service they have provided to humankind, the car has left an undeniable wake of ugliness and devastation in its path.

Lastly, we have yet to consider all the natural terrain, the woods, mountains, fields, rivers, and native habitats of the earth that have been irrevocably obliterated, plowed through, and covered with concrete or asphalt so a road could be made leading to somewhere we weren't willing to walk to. There is something egomaniacal about how we have altered the landscape of this country, and others around the planet, according to our own selfish plans and desires, against the will and to the detriment of the planet and humanity, as well as diverse cultures, species, and lifeforms.

Our lofty and imperialistic visions of glory—leading from open-ended conquest to global soul slaughter through the advanced developments of technology—have eclipsed any caring we might have for a natural world that has absolutely no use for our ways, and which is every moment being eaten away by the corrosive impact of our modern society.

And so kids play in the streets because there are no more woods or fields to play in, or they just stay in the house and remain sedentary, *playing* video games, staring at the TV, or surfing the internet. Most of us have to drive a motor vehicle to get to the park or beach—environments in which we can exercise our bodies—because we don't have much space or freedom to move around where we live. The backyard is usually too small to even get up a good run—that's if you even have a backyard. Most of us live in apartment complexes or townhomes that are all crammed together, built right alongside busy roads, next to strip malls and businesses, with very few open spaces.

It's nearly impossible to escape the grasp of industrial capitalism that surrounds us. We have literally so little open space left to wander through, to experience a little nature, a little true freedom, a little mystery and natural untainted beauty. Wherever we go, it seems we are assailed by roads with speeding cars, and by billboards and businesses that reduce human beings to consumers. It leaves me wondering, "What has become of our *humanity*?"

AS A RESULT OF OUR VILIFICATION of nature, and in our quest to keep our bodies somewhat active and *in shape*, many of us resort to acquiring memberships at twenty-four hour fitness centers to maintain a regular exercise regime in nice, safe, and sterile man-made environments—where we don't have to deal with any unruly nature stuff like dirt or bugs! Maybe sometime soon our scientists will figure out how we can exercise without sweating so we don't have to get "dirty" at all! How ironic and truly hideous that in our society we have had to privatize—for the benefit of enterprising capitalists—and cordon off chunks of space that are suitable for us to exercise our bodies, that the world we have constructed is now in many ways an inappropriate and unsafe place for humans to *play*—yes, adults play too; all the indoor gym exercise and workout activity is just another way for us to enjoy being in our bodies.

It's frustrating and sad that we live in a society which has re-created the world with such strong antithesis to nature and our natural state of being, in which our bodies have lost their importance in relation to man-made machines and industry, and in which consumerism now exceeds our own human freedoms and well-being. Indeed, it seems we have lost touch with the spiritual dimensions of nature and our bodies altogether. So why has this happened?

In the first place, historically speaking, the European-Christian-pilgrim-become-American has held an attitude of antithesis towards nature all along, viewing nature more as a threatening force that must be overcome and subverted than as a nurturing and creative—albeit challenging—environment of which we are a part, and to which we belong. We certainly have expressed little interest in discerning the revelation, as the eloquent and insightful East-West philosopher Alan Watts surmises, that "the individual is so interwoven with the universe that he and it are one body."

Quite to the contrary, we have inherited a habitual form of perception in which we view ourselves primarily in terms of our vulnerability and subsequent compensatory superiority to nature—as well as to Native American and indigenous peoples—instead of viewing nature as an ally and co-participant in life.

Placing ourselves as a combatant to nature—as well as a combatant to our own inner nature revealing itself in the form of our impulses, urges, instincts, and *irrational desires*—we've taken it upon ourselves to shape and mold the natural world such that it fits in with our *rational ideas* of how it can best suit us. We've interacted with nature in the spirit of domination, contorting it for our own benefit—while also contorting our own inner selves—thereby distancing ourselves from an authentic encounter with nature.

By creating artificial and distorted relationships with nature, we've also accomplished the same thing in our relationships, not only with one another, but within ourselves, *with our own true inner nature*—because, much as we try, we cannot ever truly separate our *inner* nature, of which we are inherently composed, from the *outer* nature that surrounds us. Although, as Alan Watts was fond of pointing out, there can be no "inside" without an "outside," no "me" without a "you," the idea that we can separate our own "inner" human nature from our "outer" natural surroundings—which literally permeate through us as a living environment—remains the great hoax of modern life!

Although I've stated the following perspective in various ways, it remains a central thesis of my overall argument, of my assertion about the true nature, and thus purpose, of human beings: *hu-*

man beings belong in nature, because we are nature. When we remove ourselves from nature, we become less human. This creates a problematic state of affairs that is now threatening to destroy us via ecological devastation which—because we are part of the ecology—is also human devastation. Indeed, the environmental crisis is the outer manifestation of an inner, unarticulated crisis of soul in which we've abandoned, contorted, and disabled our innermost precious selves, the native, natural human beings that we are.

It is our great mistake and self-deception to think that we are somehow above the world of nature, that we can control Her as we would a pet—as though it were our secret desire to recreate the whole functioning order of life *in our own image*. Although we can never do this, we keep trying because we believe—in our grandiose, self-serving mode of thinking—that we can do just about anything we want to do without regard for the impact on the world around us.

This is perhaps the main difference between modern and ancient perspectives, between Western and pre-Western models and modes of being: the pre-Western paradigm affirms cooperation, empathy, mutuality, respect, and interrelated interdependence as prime values or standards of living; whereas the modern Western paradigm asserts dominance, control, manipulation, disregard, segregation, and nonrelated independence as our main guiding principles.

This point of view is the origin of our main sickness, a sickness of the soul, a psychological isolation. Speaking about the modern paradigm from an indigenous perspective, Martin Prechtel states:

> It was nature, wildness, this undomesticated spirit that fled when it got enslaved, insulted, maimed, beaten or scared off. This trespass on one's personal nature or soul

is what Mayan shamans considered the prime source of illness to humans.

I, for one, don't want to live *above* nature, *beside* nature, *separate* from nature, or in ways that control and contort nature, so that She becomes deformed and insane, and dies. The modern way of living distrusts nature, as we distrust each other and ourselves. Living in this way, we have become a sick people: depressed, frantic, anxiety-ridden, greedy, cruel, alienated, suicidal, power-hungry, afraid, unfulfilled and lonely.

Most of us have been prescribed some kind of anti-depressant, anti-anxiety, anti-psychotic, anti-hyperactivity, *anti-reality* medication, and/or engage in psychiatry, psychotherapy or some form of emotional-behavioral-cognitive readjustment regime just to cope with our crazy lives, just to retain some form of stability or sanity in this mad, dark world.

Welcome to America: "Land of the free and home of the brave!"

We've created lives of false dysfunctional separation from nature and from one another. We live inside separate boxes cut off from the natural world and from our fellow man, keeping us safe, private, protected, and comfortable, but also detached, miserable, lonely, and meaningless. We think we have conquered nature and are creating an ideal world, but we've really only conquered ourselves, our instincts, our needs, our inherent humanity, and our interrelated unity with the universe.

In just one hundred years we've accomplished so much ecological damage it is almost unspeakable! The majority of us live structured, boring lives, anxiety-stricken and numbed. We've learned to manage and control ourselves so well that we've had to invent "amusement parks"—as well as countless enthralling, adrenalin pumping video games, cyber games, television shows, and action-packed movies glorifying violence—so that we can safely or vicariously "lose control" and *scare ourselves into feeling alive again.*

WHEN I WAS A KID, we lived on a dirt and gravel road in the country. Across the street was a huge cow pasture with a big, old picturesque red barn, and surrounding our small horse-shoe shaped housing development were corn fields and woods, through which we kids constantly romped, played, and were sensuously entranced. In the winter, we skated on the small iced-over pond in the woods and sled down snowy hills all day long. During the summer, we rode our bikes, climbed trees, and hung out in the secretive tree fort we were forever building in the woods. We also played a lot of dumb, old fashioned games outside, like Kick The Can.

As a kid, my friends and I were virtually free and unconstrained by the development of industry, of concrete and steel and the suburban stranglehold which has encumbered and encompassed much of the open land these days. We were also free from the oppressions and seductions of technology and modes of virtual entertainment that are so nauseatingly pervasive today.

Later in my early adolescence, my family moved to three acres of pristine woods. We lived in what seemed like a Tarzan World, with huge, crazy, hairy vines hanging from tall trees that were thickly grown upon with all kinds of ivy. The land was brambling with a myriad forms of green plant growth, inhabited by deer, rabbits, squirrels, and snakes. The flies, measuring nearly an inch long, looked like they buzzed out of an ancient and monstrous world. There was also lots of poison ivy and masses of a sprawling plant that had sharp, arrow-like protuberances all along its stem and leaves which would quickly scratch, scrape, and tear one's skin—we called this nuisance plant "arrowroot."

We hacked into this land with machetes, axes, and chainsaws, clearing enough to build a small home, and did a lot of landscaping and gardening as well, working the land much of the year. We grew tons of tomatoes which, after picking, we would place on the high deck railing until inevitably some would begin to rot, at which point we'd throw them at the trees, reveling in the "splat" that a good shot would produce. Living in the wild woods entailed much hot, onerous, and "dirty" work which I dreaded at the time, but upon reflection, I think something of the spirit of that land got into me.

Now I live in a modern city, with its concrete sidewalks, asphalt roads, constant cars and traffic, buildings of plaster and steel, and merchants like 7-11 and Jack In The Box—a world far removed from that of my childhood. The harsh tranquility of nature carries healing energy that enables one to feel the potent mystery of one's existence and a deep sense of ancient belonging to the earth. People who have only lived in the city have difficulty relating to or imagining this.

The man-made world is quite different than the world of nature—city life is engaging, stimulating, and often times overwhelming, but living in the midst of nature reveals that there is more to life than man's creations and concerns which are highlighted in the life of the city.

In the city, our awareness is severely limited to our own regulated and controlled experiment of life, "safe from beasts and vermin," outside the domain of nature, but really plastered and bolted on top of nature in our spirit of domination. As such, it can be a positive environment in which we have the opportunity to experience human culture in a concentrated form. However, without the ample influx of nature, we inevitably forget who we are and transform into aberrations of humanity such as can be witnessed every night on the local news.

Our attempts to incorporate nature into city-life are sometimes ridiculous and absurd; note the trees we've planted which grow up through metal grates in the sidewalk. What a tragic and sad image is this! The trees look tortured because they don't belong growing up through small holes whose visage foretells an early death, the metal grates surrounded by cement which is stained and scarred with dark remnants of gum, food, cigarettes, random graffiti, and trash. This kind of inflicted deformity of nature by man is morbid. To top it all off, we plant the trees in a symmetrical, linear fashion, thereby obliterating their native wildness.

Sometimes, we put in narrow strips of grass between the sidewalk and the road. As a younger man, I used to walk almost exclusively on these strips of grass because it felt so much better on my feet to feel the grass instead of the concrete. But, of course, the strips of grass are really only for show, for looking at, or allowing your dog to sniff around and take a pee; a respectable citizen knows that they are expected to walk on the sidewalk, that their urges to trample upon the green grass and to feel its soft resilient ground beneath their feet should be duly repressed.

The real earth is just too messy for us *superior human beings* who have, through our need for social conformity, sublimated our instincts to actually contact, touch, or walk upon the earth. Sadly, we reserve that denigration for the lower-class farmers and laborers—mainly *illegals*—who do our lawn work and gardening.

It seems that every day we tear down more nature—both in the United States and in other countries—turning wild lands into housing developments, strip malls, and areas of industry. According to the environmental protection group Raintree:

In 1950, about 15 percent of the Earth's land surface was covered by rainforest. Today, more than half has already gone up in smoke. In fewer than fifty years, more than half of the world's tropical rainforests have fallen victim to fire and the chain saw, and the rate of destruction is still accelerating. Unbelievably, *more than 200,000 acres of rainforest are burned every day.* That is more than 150 acres lost every minute of every day, and 78 million acres lost every year! More than 20 percent of the Amazon rainforest is already gone, and much more is severely threatened as the destruction continues. It is estimated that the Amazon alone is vanishing at a rate of 20,000 square miles a year. *If nothing is done to curb this trend, the entire Amazon could well be gone within fifty years.*

These statistics are mind-blowing! One wonders how it is possible for humankind to destroy so much land so quickly. According to Vicki Ilene, a writer for the website *Love to Know*:

The United States deforestation has caused the destruction of virgin forests by 90 percent since 1600. At the rate of deforestation currently in the United States, only one-fourth of the forests standing today will be standing in 70 years.

MODERN HUMANKIND HAS BECOME a blind beast, hungry and raving, perpetually devouring nature, greedily altering it into something that only serves itself. When will we stop? Or will we? I thank God for those few exceptionally compassionate human beings, like Sasha Butterfly, who devote their lives to safeguarding the planet. The term "tree-hugger" is often used by opponents of ecological protection—as well as dumb, drunk guys at the bar—in a snide and deprecating way intended to insult those of us who would dare to show one ounce of affection for trees, plants, and animals. But if you feel no care or love for the world of nature, chances are you feel no care or love for anything other than your own myopic material existence.

Where have our hearts gone in this modern anti-earth world? What has happened to our human instinct for compassion, to that place inside all of us that recognizes the lives of others as the same as our own? The inner sanctity of universal compassion, intimations of our ultimate unity with all life, has been bought and sold by capitalism, has faded away, to be only occasionally glimpsed in rare moments of shared, communal tragedy such as the events of 9-11-2001.

There is no doubt that we are quickly consuming the planet, just as the beast of capitalism consumes our own souls. For in our consumer society, consumption is our main concern. It's consume or be consumed. We take, take, take from the earth and what we give back is pollution, smog, trash, litter, ugliness, and devastation. Why do we only take the good and only give back the bad? We are not *making the world a better place* by destroying it.

Recently, however, it has become more widely recognized that care and love for the planet may be an essential activity for humanity if we wish to continue to live upon it for much longer. Somehow we need to shake our attitude of enslaving the earth to meet our own whims; we must rejoin her generative energies in ways in which we reciprocate the gift of life and not horde it all for ourselves.

We've got to realize that we are not alone on this planet, and expand our awareness of the other earthly life forms—beings that are essential for a harmonious process of existence. We've got to understand this not only with our heads; *we must remember how to feel it in our bodies and souls*, to somehow recognize our inseparability from the ecosystems and energies of the earth. It wouldn't really be all that hard if we weren't conditioned by an exclusively technology-driven materialist world to live in isolation from nature.

There is a recent commercial that ends with the slogan: "Building a smarter planet." This sounds like some kind of global genetic engineering project. The phrase, in and of itself, is the epitome of egomaniacal megalomania! First of all, we did not build this planet to begin with, but the idea that we can illustrates our sense of world domination, as if we are the new gods. The planet itself is remarkably intelligent, whereas humankind has shown itself to be, in many ways, stupid and insane—especially when we, as a collective species, contribute daily to killing the planet.

But back to the slogan.

Is the idea that we need to "build a smarter planet" because the original planet was not smart enough to handle all our modern waste, pollution, deforestation, and myriad forms of devastation? Perhaps we just need to build a tougher planet, like a Ford truck! Will our "smarter planet" be an all man-made planet, built just for ourselves, with mechanical butterflies and virtual grass, our brains wired into a gigantic communal computer terminal?

If every possible human experience could be preprogrammed, wouldn't that make humanity infinitely safer, more predictable and controllable—albeit creatively dead, pathetic, and sordid? We could form committees, representatives of humanity like the house and the senate that choose what experiences will be programmed into the grand central station of our communal computer brains. But then again, wouldn't these representatives already have had their brains pre-programmed as well?

Uh oh! This could turn into a nasty experiment: the deranged manipulating the deranged. Gee, it's beginning to look a lot like Christmas—a lot like how our society already functions. If only we could do away with the human capacity for instinct and impulse altogether, once and for all. Then we'd have EVERY-THING under control!

If we are to initiate a kind of *re-attunement* to the forces of nature and to more cooperative ways of life, we could learn much from the original inhabitants of this land. In Malcolm Margolin's book, *The Way We Lived*, the Pomo Indians of California tell us:

> Plants are thought to be alive, their juice is their blood and they grow. The same is true of trees. All things die, therefore all things have life. Because all things have life, gifts have to be given to all things.

Native American tribes maintained reciprocal, symbolic, ritual relationships with the spirit powers of animals and plants—as with the stars, sun, and moon—in which they gave back something of what they had gained in the hunt or the harvest as a gesture of appreciation and goodwill, and so that they might receive again. In this way, these societies attempted to demonstrate their thankfulness and humility to the spirits of nature. By realizing they were at the mercy of the natural world, they developed respect and regard for its powers to bless or curse them, and thereby also engendered compassionate relationships with nature. Their lives were intrinsically interwoven with the lives of other "beings" who comprise this mystery planet.

We moderns, however, have taken the whole matter into our own hands. We manipulate the nature powers, calculating and judging our survival plans according to our own separatist rationale and reasoning. We don't view animals, trees and plants as having spirits—or any intrinsic value in their own right—that we could engage with in some kind of sacred or reciprocal relationship. In fact, we deprecate animals by insinuating degrading connotations upon the very word "animal."

As the self-proclaimed "masters of the universe," we're entrained to *view the world as our oyster*. Thus, *we own the animals and plants*, or we buy them once their lives have been taken—and we have little thought or care for the lives of these *beings* that sustain us.

Consideration for the lives of animals and plants is a way of thinking that has been "built out" of our way of life. We think of our lives in terms of objectified material survival, of how much money we can make to buy all that we need and want. Very few of us have a hand in procuring these items through hunting, growing, crafting, or building the things we need, which instead we work to make money to pay for.

Unlike indigenous cultures, we have very little relationship to the *source* of our lives. Because we purchase what we need or want, we have an abstract and distant relationship to these things, and we tend to have little understanding of, or interest in, their origins or nature.

OCTAVIO PAZ WAS A MEXICAN writer and poet. In 1961, he wrote *The Labyrinth of Solitude,* an excellent and poetic portrayal of the personal and social struggles of Mexicans to maintain their identity under the immense and calamitous pressures of the Spanish Invasion, up through 20th Century North American impact. He describes the difference in attitude and way of life between Americans—intent on fully realizing their potential state of modernity—and Mexicans, who struggle to somehow retain elements of their traditional culture in the face of such pressures:

> Man is alone everywhere. But the solitude of the Mexican, under the great stone night of the high plateau that is

still inhabited by insatiable gods, is very different from that of the North American who wanders in an abstract world of machines, fellow citizens and moral precepts. In the valley of Mexico, man feels himself suspended between heaven and earth, and he oscillates between contrary powers and forces, and petrified eyes, and devouring mouths. Reality—that is, the world around us—exists by itself here, has a life of its own, and was not invented by man as it was in the United States. The Mexican feels himself to have been torn from the womb of this reality, which is both creative and destructive, both Mother and Tomb. He has forgotten the word that ties him to all those forces through which life manifests itself. Therefore he shouts or keeps silent, stabs or prays, or falls asleep for a hundred years.

Paz' description of the Mexican who still feels a profound connection with the original reality of the earth, and yet also feels somehow estranged from it, portrays the pain and confusion of a person with an internal indigenous paradigm who has been subverted and incorporated into a modern way of life. Paz' portrayal expresses a true sense of the experience of nature as a spiritual reality—a living, powerful, perhaps divine reality that *spat man out* upon the surface of things to have his own reckoning with Itself.

When Paz states, "Reality ... exists by itself here, has a life of its own, and was not invented by man," there is the implication that the Mexican does not perceive himself to be fully in control of the situation or "running the show," but, rather, places himself in a kind of interdependent *relationship* with the powers of life-nature-universe, in which he experiences the awesomeness of his participation in life and death.

This relationship and perspective of being a part of something larger and autonomous from himself seems to have been lost by modern man. I believe it is this experience, grounded in the spiritual reality of nature, that is needed to heal us from our current state of fragmentation.

XI

VIOLENCE AS ENTERTAINMENT

"The gods have become diseases ..."
~C. G. Jung, *Collected Works, Vol. 13*

I AM REPEATEDLY STRUCK by our country's incredible capacity for criminalization and incarceration, our unending fascination with criminal court proceedings—such as Judge Judy and the televised trials of famous persons like OJ—, and the rise of TV shows about criminal investigations and prison life, such as CSI Miami, Women Behind Bars, and weekend-long MSNBC "Lock-Up" documentaries. We have become a culture completely obsessed with all aspects of crime and punishment, with law enforcement, the "justice" system, and *violence as entertainment*. Every night we look on with a mixture of horror, disbelief, and glee as the TV news features the latest crime, the latest high speed chase, the latest indictment, and the latest ruling or prison sentence.

The fact is, these kinds of news stories fascinate us.

But why?

Does life in a modern technological world breed individuals who are more criminally incited or inclined?

Is it somehow more difficult for us to cope with our lives, with our basic instincts and needs, in societies which are cut off from nature? Through disconnecting and dividing us from our true instinctual inner nature, has modern technological society distorted and deformed our souls into criminal forms of madness? Or does our high level of sensationalizing interest in crime and punishment—in *violence as entertainment*—point to something else?

The list of television shows based on crime and criminal investigation which one can watch on any given night is too long to list. It is simply mind-blowing. In fact, these kinds of TV shows dominate the air waves, and it is sometimes difficult to find a program on a major channel that is not focused on criminal matters, that does not feature the lethal wielding of a gun or depict a bloody and cruel mortification of the body.

Is this *criminally obsessed* "state of the media" a projection of our own guilty conscience, social anxieties, and mistrust of an expandingly impersonal, mechanized, and out-of-control world? If so, is it also a kind of reflection of the true "state of the union" in which we live, and thereby intended to help us adapt to the chaos of *the real world*?

Perhaps our interest in crime and prosecution is indicative of our interest in power and control, things we desperately need as a result of how powerless and out of control we actually feel in this society of surveillance and increasing impingement on our individual liberties and freedoms.

Does our love of crime, prosecution, and violence as entertainment, both in reality—as in the news—and at the movies, reveal a secret wish we harbor for living the exciting and dangerous lives of criminals, police, or FBI agents?

Through vicariously experiencing their thoughts, motivations, feelings, and actions at the cinema are we relieved of our own pent up frustrations and feelings of vengeance at having been sharply instructed on what we can and cannot do, can or cannot feel or want, by our parents, teachers, bosses, government officials, and law enforcement—at having been socially repressed—our whole lives?

Or are we simply *taken* by the archetypal dynamics of the pursuer and the pursued, the hunter and the hunted, the triangulation of criminal, victim, and prosecutor?

What inner psychological need is met through our mass obsession with crime and prosecution?

We revel at the movies when the criminal gets away with the perfect crime, just as we revel at the news upon hearing of real life criminals—be they ex-football players, politicians, or just ordinary citizens—who are convicted of the crimes they committed and sentenced to years in prison. Either way, we love to see people roll the dice with their lives.

In fact, we seem to rely on these people and their dramas to make us feel more alive, more pumped with adrenalin and filled with energy. Perhaps the dramas of their lives shake us from the numbing boredom of our own.

WHEN I FIRST SAW the television show COPS, I was working at a group home for troubled teens. The teens really got into this show and viewed it often as one of their favorites. They expressed vocal, guttural, and emotional reactions as the burglar was chased through back yards and eventually brought down by the COPS. I never liked this show. To me, it seemed ridiculous because it portrayed our society celebrating its own disgrace and demise, dressing up the tragedy of crime as a kind of entertainment.

But the teenagers loved it. I guess they more easily placed themselves into the dramas and dynamics of cops and robbers, of police and criminals, of the persecuting authority figure nabbing the bad guy, who, like themselves, was a sort of outlaw living on the fringes of society. Perhaps they unconsciously identified with the criminal who, through his or her transgressions against the rules and norms of society, became a victim of the justice system, became condemned, labeled as a "convict," and sentenced into a life of incarceration and surveillance that was akin to life in a group home as a teenager.

Many of these teenagers had been abused or abandoned by their parents and were, at various stages, working through their guilt, anger, and grief. They had been victimized as children, which in turn had driven many of them to become misfits and outcasts, maladjusted in schools and in society at large. Due to these factors, I could understand how these youth might more easily relate to the COPS show, but for the everyday, normal American this overwhelming interest in crime alludes me.

Perhaps the Freudians are right, and everything does boil down to our collective struggle with repressed aggression and sexuality. Freud talked about the enormity of these instincts; by the looks of our movies and our current rate of crime and incarceration, it appears as if he was correct.

More than crime alone, our society is completely engrossed by all kinds of expressions of aggression, from military maneuvers and wars, to movies, sports, angry talk show radio hosts, and heavy metal music. If aliens were to descend upon our planet and view humanity, including all the media we produce, they'd no doubt be impressed by our propensity to beat, punch, slash, shoot, maim, and murder one another—as well as crash cars and blow shit up!

Murder and brutality as entertainment betray a deep inner collective shadow of rage that we hide from one another beneath our social niceties, politenesses, and deceptive personas. It is, in fact, overwhelmingly difficult for us to be honest with one another about what we're really feeling, what we're really thinking, fantasizing, desiring, or fearing.

Ironically, people who fantasize or daydream are often deprecated for wasting their time by being lazy, not accomplishing anything, or simply engaging in an escape from reality. Yet those who watch TV all night are not. Perhaps, this is because in our culture we are conditioned from birth to become someone we are not, to feel what we don't feel and not feel what we do, to think what others want us to think, to stop daydreaming and to want only that which is socially sanctioned.

No wonder we're so drawn to displays of aggression; we're fed up with being oppressed! Acts of violence enable us to feel vicariously freed from the invisible cage of our lives, if only for a moment.

It seems as though we've grown numb by means of our dull lives of classroom education, offices, suburban living, and a way of life that focuses on the head, the brain, the concept, the idea, the intellect and the ego; alongside a sly refusal of our instincts, our human heart, the knowledge in our guts, our intuition, and the *natural inner animal*, the bodily senses, inner impulses and drives, the creative and spontaneous mystery that we are.

Even this process of communication through the written word is a form of abstraction, of symbolic expression that has been assigned meaning, almost arbitrarily, by humankind.

Words *refer* to real things, to ideas, feelings, objects, and interactions. However, as the old Zen masters say, "words are fingers pointing to the moon," which is to say that talking about a steak will not fill our bellies.

Words cannot replace experience or who we are, just as reading about geography is not the same as walking around and actually exploring physical terrain. Ultimately, the body and its life cannot be replaced by concepts.

ALTHOUGH SOME WOULD SAY that it is only through applying the mandates of the mind upon the impulses of the body that any kind of social order or cultural harmony can be attained whatsoever, it appears that disembodied cultures such as our own, whose inherent impulses tend to be more repressed, are more apt to orient towards crime and punishment, as well as violence as entertainment.

In this sense, an interest in crime would indicate an unconscious attempt to resolve the intolerable situation of our collective societal repressions, which include a displacement of the body from its central role as mediator between self and world to a third party position of objectification, in which it is mainly viewed as a nuisance, or as something which we must merely keep in good repair and maintain—like a house or a car.

The essence of crime, in theory, is the presence of something devious or deviant to the normal functioning of the individual or the society. A crime is defined as an aberrant act of rebellion, a going against the grain, a transgression of laws that we hold to be essential to the sanity or sanctity of human society. Therefore, a crime is an attack on the principle of Logos, which signifies order, logic, and reason.

Perhaps this is another way of understanding our obsession with crime and violence. Because Logos—"the rational principle"—has become so ubiquitous in its rule over our lives, crime and violence as entertainment have arisen as compensatory functions in our attempts to cope with the utter obliteration of our instincts, or the principle of Eros—which I take to refer moreover to love and the passions of the heart, the soul, and the body than to only sexual desire.

When the body, the instincts, the passions, and our innate spiritual desires for a deeper and more fulfilling kind of communion with life and the world of others is denied us by our culture, crime and violence become attractive alternatives.

Through acts of crime and violence, the impenetrable walls of restriction—by which we are sequestered from our true wholeness—are violated and temporarily destroyed, thereby allowing us to make connection with portions of ourselves and the world with which we are normally disallowed by the rule of Logos—or what Freud called the superego. Just as drugs and alcohol can also give us glimpses into areas of our personality and dimensions of the world beyond our normal and socially regulated purview, crime and violence—when they are committed as ritual acts against the arbitrary rule of order—provide us with a momentary sense of freedom and release from consensual restrictions.

Upon more extensive analysis, it can be seen that our societal fascination with crime as entertainment is really a calling to address the deeper needs of the human spirit that are chronically and habitually repressed by the ruling paradigm of our society. Ironically, the same society that denies us the full and fulfilling expression and experience of our deeper instincts also has attempted to rectify this denial through condoning our vicarious enjoyment of violence as entertainment. Yet the degree to which violence in the media is pronounced also belies an underlying disenchantment with it.

Although we may be perpetually drawn to that which is taboo, the way we drink from the fountain of bloodshed and violence—whether at the movies or news of the latest war or murder trial—is rather morbid, and should alert us to wondering why we have become so numb as to have to continually shock ourselves into feeling anything at all.

Asking ourselves what it is that we truly need, I think we will find that we need *to feel*.

We need to feel alive.

And we need to feel connected to ourselves and to the world. We need to feel the healing presence of the earth, of nature, and the magic of being alive. We need to live in some kind of harmony with our instincts and find meaningful ways of expressing who we are. Lastly, we need to live in an authentic and nourishing interrelationship with the social world around us.

Violence as entertainment is truly a form of diversion, both a cleverly symbolic reflection of, and distraction from, the state of our own tormented souls. Although violence as entertainment appears to be a good way to wake us up, it is truly a meager way of living. Violations of any kind are really desperate attempts at connection, just as drunk guys fighting in a bar are secretly striving to have some kind of fulfilling camaraderie.

But living vicariously through actors who shoot one another, or through criminals who break the law, is just another way of avoiding your life, of refusing to take responsibility for your own desires or to live in accord with your own true nature.

XII

SOUL CONTROL

I AM ALWAYS SURPRISED when someone asks me how I am—and I give an honest response about feeling anything other than "fine," "okay," or "great," for instance, sad, depressed, or angry—that their typical reaction is to attempt to talk me out of feeling what I'm feeling, to instill me with hope or optimism, and to basically "help me feel good." I appreciate the typical person's response as a form of caring, but it also insults my integrity as they seek to deny my authentic and true emotional state which obviously pertains to my own unique life situation and internal psychological reality. Their response assumes that I either want to feel *better*, that I *should* want to feel better, or that *I should feel better.*

Such responses are innately invalidating of a person's experience. They express unconscious collective judgments about human beings that are harmful and limiting to a person's potential—let alone their needs for acceptance. Sometimes, such responses even make me wonder if the person would rather me be someone I am not.

Often times, when I ask other people how they are, and they happen to be not doing or feeling incredibly well, they start off by saying something like, "Well I can't complain ..." When I tell the person that they can complain, they usually laugh, then drop down beneath their ingrained layer of self-recrimination for having feelings that they believe they shouldn't have and begin to talk about what's really going on with them. Ironically, much of what is difficult about feelings is not the feelings themselves, but that *we think we're not supposed to feel them.*

I sometimes wonder why we are so conditioned to refuse, reject and deny who we are: our feelings which express our depths and complexity, and our pain. In an age of such profound social, political, and economic repercussions, can we afford to continue to deceive others about something as significant as the state of our souls? About the underlying psychology of our humanity that interactively affects the greater precarious world which we are attempting to heal?

Hollywood seems to recognize how emotionally repressed we are and capitalizes on this, over and over again, with the same basic plots that, at their best, involve dramatic emotional expression of the kind of real human struggles that we usually try to hide from one another in everyday life. Artists and actors are able, allowed, and encouraged to express their emotions creatively. Musicians, poets, and artists transform their emotions, including the suffering and pathos of life, through their selected medium into forms that translate both pain and pleasure into something inspiring, beautiful or otherwise meaningful—and at times numinous.

Transforming pain into beauty or inspiration is part of the human potential which can only occur through embracing darkness, tragedy, fear, and suffering. However, pain and pleasure, good and bad, and positive and negative are mainly polarizing concepts, subjective interpretations, not objective absolutes. Because they are concepts and matters of perspective, they can be transcended.

There is a way of experiencing life not in terms of its contradictions, but in terms of its wholeness, a way in which all things are equally considered, in which both pain and pleasure, heartache and inspiration, and happiness and sadness are all accepted, and come together to form a greater reality.

The mystical Persian poet Jelaluddin Rumi referred to this state of being:

> Out beyond ideas of right-doing and wrong-doing
> there is a field. I will meet you there.

If we are to live authentic lives in integrity with ourselves, we will have to acknowledge all our complexity and depth, including the conflicted and confused areas of our personalities. However challenging this may prove to be, society will likely retain its own opinion about what is acceptable and what is not. If we are honest with ourselves, we'll discover that who we are is not always the person society wants us to be. In the eyes of the world, sometimes who we really are is not acceptable, and this makes it difficult to be true to ourselves.

The forging of a strong sense of self may require great perseverance in the face of adversary, through a series of rejections or malodious judgments from others which we may experience as fiery, sharp, stinging burns. If we have the discipline to realize that our society comes replete with preconceived, preprogrammed negative projections which it will arbitrarily place upon us, we may gain the greater inner awareness to move beyond social conventions of right and wrong. At times, remaining committed to one's own fate, one's own truth or sense of virtue—and doing what one knows one must do—may require walking through blazing fires of recrimination from others.

Look at what the historical Jesus went through in affirming his own view of God and reality—he was crucified. In so doing, he maintained integrity with himself and his life mission. He also illustrated the credo "To thine own self be true."

At every turn, the world tells us who we should be, how we should act, and what we should want. Many of these demanding messages are impelled by capitalistic endeavors; how can we trust a society that really only wants the contents of our wallets? Growing up, we're told we should go to college if we want to be "successful," so that we can get a good job and a good paycheck. We're inculcated with the premise that education is mandatory if we want to be materially or socially successful, and if we really want to *fit in* with society and play a respectable role.

This premise, however, is only the beginning of what we're told we need to do to become, and remain, respectable and successful in the eyes of society. It's another way society tells us that who we are in our natural state of being *is not good enough*, that who we are needs to be continually improved, trained, or otherwise altered through societal institutions—many of which are money-grubbing capitalist endeavors—to become and remain of value to the world.

Upon graduation from high school, we are instructed either to go to college or into the military, so that we can "make something of ourselves." We are to enlist in one social institution or the other, really to benefit this capitalistic society. Either we devote our future earnings to paying back loans for a college education, or we risk sacrificing our lives for the country in support of military maneuvers that have been led by genius minds such as George W. Bush! Either way, the world wants to keep tabs on us, especially our finances.

Upon release from high school—which is seen as our final step from childhood into adulthood and a potentially independent life—according to the options with which we are advised by parents, school officials, and media, we are strongly encouraged to embark upon conventional and socially sanctioned paths to continue to develop social power, respect, success, status, and rank. There is little room or allowance within these options for us to walk our own chosen path outside of the normal and expected protocol, for a journey of individuation based upon free choice, innovation, and our own unique vision. Most of us who can afford to do so engage upon the customary path of higher education in hopes of a fantastic future and on a search for self-discovery.

Once the degree is attained, we are motivated to rush into a chosen occupation so that we are able to begin to re-pay our monetary debt to the college or to the government from whom we obtained the loans to attend the college—the government and higher education are two institutions that get a lot of action sleeping in bed with each other! If we do not immediately begin to repay the debt, it only increases with interest. In this manner, now that we have proven ourselves successful as young, ambitious, and intelligent adults, society has arranged a built-in mechanism in which *they now begin to own us financially.*

And this is only the beginning.

Next comes the car loan and car insurance, the cell phone bill, the rent, the credit card, and eventually the home loan. In order to participate in all the wonderful, lovely, extravagant features of the modern world, we become chained to it by the many tethers of monetary debt. This ensures that we will keep on working harder than ever to keep up with the bills. We are thus controlled and owned by the many merchants of capitalism, spending the rest of our lives as "glorified indentured servants" with limited materialistic liberties.

That's America, "Land of the free."

In these ways, we are subtly, but surely, manipulated to trade our freedom for servitude. Someone who is free is not owned, either by the bank or by the media that advertises *countless things that are of utmost necessity for you to purchase in order to enjoy your life and be successful.*

What can be said about the soul of a society in which one's participation and belonging come hand in hand with a payment plan? With endless obligations that mandate a life of servitude and work? The underlying truth is that to belong to this culture you must sacrifice your freedom; to be a member you must pay the life-long dues.

The United States makes the prodigious proclamation that we are "The home of the brave and the land of the free." But are we really? Bravery is a state of possessing great courage and demonstrating one's valor through actions that involve the risk of one's own well-being for the well-being of others. Perhaps it takes bravery just to step out of the house and into the madness of the streets, or to go to work at a job which rarely, if ever, cares one iota about your soul. However, when I look around me, I don't exactly see brave people, but moreover people going along with the general constructed plan of society. I see fearful and inhibited people, frantic, impatient, sometimes joyous people ... but not really "brave."

As for being "free," it seems most people are incredibly busy and overly occupied working to earn enough cash to pay the bills and keep up with the material demands of living in the 21st Century New World Order. Worrying about *freedom*, we think, is for third world countries and primitive peoples who haven't yet adopted our *enlightened* form of capitalistic and democratic society.

When the soul control that the world inflicts upon us descends into the inner reaches of our emotions we risk becoming completely altered into someone who we are not. We may be forced to do many things in order to maintain our status as functioning members of society—like going to work at whatever job we can get, which we may dislike—yet, when we are manipulated to disguise our inner feelings, the constitution of our hearts and souls, how can we continue to make believe that we are really who we say we are?

In the final analysis, perhaps it is always risky to reveal ourselves, to be who we really are and say what we really feel instead of resorting to telling people we feel fine when we feel terrible, or that we are happy when we really feel sad or empty. For in the assertion of our true self and our real voice lies the only hope of redeeming a society of souls that are continually programmed by hierarchies of materialism bent on dominating and controlling its faithful servants.

XIII

CHRISTIAN NATION?

I HAVE HEARD IT SAID repeatedly, especially out of the mouths of politicians and religious zealots, that "America is a Christian Nation." This is stated as if such a thing was a blatant fact, regardless of the countless non-Christian peoples who are just as equally American citizens. While it is true that America has an enduring faith in Christianity via its extensive surplus of denominations, I would like to know in what specific ways our nation is strictly Christian, "Christ-like," or an exemplar of Christian principles and tenets. Indeed, what are the collective lessons of Jesus Christ that we as an American society have integrated into our daily routines?

It is said that Jesus died on the cross by crucifixion so that we mortals could be saved from our collective sins and, henceforth, be redeemed into the afterlife in the glory of God. Therefore, it would seem that two of the main teachings of Jesus were: 1) sacrifice—as in sacrificing one's participation in earthly life so that life in the next world, the eternal and divine realm, would be guaranteed—and, 2) forgiveness—for it is said that Jesus forgave freely those who bore false witness against him and made a mockery of his teachings, as well as those who ridiculed and eventually murdered him.

The essential distillation of the sacrifice and forgiveness associated with Jesus' crucifixion appears to be one of overcoming the ego, or concerns about oneself, in order to bring well-being and wholeness to the world of others. Another aspect of the teachings of Jesus appears to be that of universal compassion—as in "Love thy neighbor"—or love for all people, including persons of every race, gender, and social class.

For, as we are told, Jesus died on the cross to redeem all of humankind, not just those who he knew personally, or who cared for and loved him.

In the living of his difficult life, Jesus also appears to have taught us something about personal integrity, as well as developing an alliance with a transcendent reality; call this God, the Cosmic Father, Truth, or a higher philosophy of living based on "selflessness" and service for the good of others. Through his life and crucifixion, Jesus appears to have maintained alignment with these principles, an unwavering trust in his higher or greater purpose, and a connection with his ultimate spiritual source.

Through a willing sacrifice of his own human life, of that which is mortal and temporal for that which is divine and eternal, Jesus taught that too much focus on materialism and this ever-changing, transitory world of things is unnecessary, and that an awareness and consideration of the eternal dimension of one's soul, or fate, is of utmost importance. Although I do not consider myself to be a Christian in the traditional sense, as one who was inculcated into Christianity as a child, I have gathered these insights from my own exposure to, and understanding of, Christianity through the years.

To summarize, in my own limited, layman point of view, Christianity encompasses values such as forgiveness, universal love, compassion, kindness, nonviolence, personal integrity, connection to a spiritual source, willingness to sacrifice the personal for the divine, and a focus on the transcendent reality and fate of one's eternal soul over that of one's temporal life on earth. Judging by today's standards, this is a rather tall order for us to live by, including those who consider the United States to be a Christian Nation.

Of course, Christianity professes many other virtues than these few which I have identified from my own personal point of view and understanding; however, I believe this is a sufficient point of reckoning from which to begin a critique of the claim in question.

If we are to continue to identify ourselves as a Christian Nation, it could prove fruitful to compare and contrast true Christian values—or Christ-like attributes—with our own current, working set of American values. Let's begin with forgiveness and ask ourselves, "How does our society emphasize the Christian virtue of forgiving others who have harmed or *trespassed against us?*"

In order to answer this question, I will start by demonstrating how we do not emphasize forgiveness. Currently, there are over 2.5 million Americans incarcerated in jails and prisons—*the percentage of the population incarcerated in the United States is dramatically higher than in any other country.* Hence, it appears that our penal system—which we also refer to as our "justice system"—severely lacks the quality of forgiveness and, instead, highlights a profound capacity for inflicting revenge through prosecution and criminalization.

Our media, as well, demonstrates a fascination with crime and the indictments perpetrated by law enforcement, and is fastidious with informing us of every heinous act imaginable that is committed, could be committed, or is alleged to have been committed everyday by ordinary citizens who have crossed over the fence of *normality* into the derelict and aberrant forms of behavior we refer to as "criminal." This is most certainly an expression of our shared social madness.

When someone has been indicted on suspicion of having committed a crime, all the various media representatives arrive on the spot like vultures to carrion, prepared to rip apart and devour the flesh of the accused, to demean and destroy them, both literally and morally, to the legal extent that they are able. And this is even before the defendant is found to be guilty. As soon as anyone becomes vulnerable to the underlying prosecutorial wrath of his fellow man—as exemplified by the media—they are quickly consumed in horrible proceedings which entail extensive and debilitating character assassination and potential life ruination.

These all too common, culturally sanctioned behaviors have nothing to do with forgiveness but, quite to the contrary, are based in a model of aggressive attack and revenge, demonstrating a profound lack of adherence to the Christian virtue of forgiveness in the United States.

Psychologically speaking, perhaps our profound consensual lack of capacity for forgiveness—as expressed by our frenzied propensity for indictment and prosecution—points towards our inability to forgive ourselves based on an underlying presence of self-guilt. For when we point an accusing finger at others there is usually an unseen finger pointing right back at ourselves. I cannot accept or love in another person what I am unable to accept or love in myself. "To err is human; to forgive is divine." But to enact revenge and torment upon one who has erred is perhaps an error in itself.

Our reactive nature towards those who have "erred" belies our own suppressed discontentment, anger, and hostility, which needs only a justifiable excuse to be released from our secret inner vault and vented upon someone who appears to deserve it. But what good does this do? In fact, this sort of reaction is not much more than a replication of the perceived transgression which instigated our own.

If we are to resolve wrong-doing, violence, or harmful behaviors, at some point the quality of compassion and forgiveness—along with an understanding of the fallible nature of being human—must enter into our awareness. At least this would seem to be a more Christian, or Christ-like, response to the many inevitable transgressions we will experience in our lifetimes, both personally and collectively.

As a military nation, we are neither forgiving nor tolerant. Did we even attempt any sort of negotiation with the Japanese after they bombed Pearl Harbor? No, we did not. In their attack upon the United States at Pearl Harbor, the Japanese killed 2,402 and wounded 1,282 American citizens. However, our response to their wrongful attack on us was to retaliate with two nuclear bombs, by which we killed approximately 140,000 Japanese in Hiroshima and 80,000 in Nagasaki—nearly a quarter of a million human beings.

The majority of the Japanese who died from these bombs were civilians who had nothing whatsoever to do with the attack on Pearl Harbor. Thousands more Japanese have suffered excruciatingly horrendous wounds and physical ailments, and more have died from the radiation fallout of these bombings since they occurred.

Our military actions over the years—from Vietnam to Iraq—have exemplified not forgiveness, but, in fact, its opposite: a severity of retaliation and punishment in the basest forms of violence, attack, slaughter and merciless killings. What would Jesus Christ—"The Prince of Peace"—say about so much murder? One of the foremost of the Ten Commandments of the Bible is: "Thou shalt not kill." And yet, almost every day the United States government condones murder in the name of war. We also lawfully execute our own citizens when they have killed. According to my understanding, Jesus Christ did not advise violence, although he himself was murdered by bloodthirsty, misanthropic individuals.

These occupational wars engendered by the United States demonstrate our preponderance for massively destructive and violent societal maneuvers based on theories of defense and protection, first from the spread of communism and, later, from global terrorist attacks. These wars enacted by our military, based on the underlying protective credo of our American nation, are not very Christian.

Lastly, as is well known, the United States was tragically attacked on 9-11-2001. Sadly, nearly 3,000 people died that day, and it is estimated that 6,000 perished in the ensuing aftermath. The dead included many Americans, but also citizens from ninety other countries. Subsequently, under the misleading guidance of George W. Bush, the United States used this attack as a justification to invade Iraq in 2003. In late 2011, over eight years later, President Barack Obama finally made good on his promise to remove all American troops from Iraq, but not before the damage had been done.

According to official American reports, there have been approximately 4,500 American deaths and over 31,000 American wounded in action as a result of this invasion and continued occupation of Iraq. In terms of the number of Americans killed, maimed, and irreparable psychologically scarred, through our own retaliatory actions we have essentially inflicted another 9-11 tragedy upon ourselves.

Reports on the Iraqi death toll pursuant to our invasion and war upon them are much higher, ranging from 100,000 to 1,000,000. These numbers confirm our enactment of a colossal revenge upon them—much like we did with the Japanese. Tragically, as it turns out, the Iraqis were not even responsible for the 9-11 attacks, as it is now understood that our invasion of Iraq was based on falsified information connecting the government of Saddam Hussein to the Al-Qaeda group held responsible for the 9-11 attacks.

So the United States murdered 100,000 to 1,000,000 Iraqi people—wounding countless others, displacing families, and inciting a general state of utter chaos, turmoil, and social nightmare to an entire country—all in the name of revenge for an act neither they nor their government committed. This is plainly anti-Christian behavior.

This kind of behavior, in purely psychological terms, is also called "projecting your shadow." The shadow is generally known as that part of our personality which we deny, repress, or hide from the world of others. Carl Jung coined the term, stating "By shadow I mean the 'negative' side of the personality, the sum of all those unpleasant qualities we like to hide ..."

But the shadow is not only a personal attribute, it also pertains to families, groups, and nations, as evidenced through a homogeneous negative regard one group has for another—such as the unquestioned enmity the U.S. and the U.S.S.R. had for one another through the long, cold war—as well as through the atrocities of actual war. Commenting on the relationship between war and the collective shadow, psychologist Sam Keen states, "The wars we engage in are compulsive rituals, shadow dramas in which we continually try to kill those parts of ourselves we deny and despise."

In the case of Iraq, the U.S. shifted blame for something horrible done to us onto them. They became the alleged culprit, as their guilt was sold to us by our politicians. In essence, we were eager to blame someone, to have a face onto which we could project our outrage and disdain. Instead of reflecting very deeply on why 9-11 occurred, we went on a reactive, frenzied killing spree.

Our war upon Iraq is probably the most recent example of our corrupt governmental responses to aggressions—perceived or actual—against our country, in which we demonstrated our supreme talent with deception of our own citizenry in order to enact revenge and the violent exercising of our military power—which in no way can be interpreted as a capacity for forgiveness, though we continually proclaim ourselves to be a "Christian Nation."

AND WHAT OF UNIVERSAL LOVE and compassion? Are we a culture that promotes these Christ-like qualities? Firstly, it must be stated that love is perhaps one of the most complex and diverse notions, celebrated and mourned down through the ages in most every culture. For purposes of this discussion, however, the point must be stressed that I am limiting my reflections of love to agape love, filial love, perhaps more well known as Platonic love, which, you may protest, is quite boring when compared with erotic love, or the love to which Plato referred when he said, "Love is a divine madness."

In the current context, however, it should be emphasized that I am speaking of universal love and compassion, or lovingkindness, known in the Buddhist tradition as metta. As such, metta is characterized in Buddhist thought as "unconditional: open and unobstructed," as "love that is not bound to desire." So then, how does our society promulgate universal or unconditional love and compassion?

Or do we?

During the holiday season, we become more charitable and many of us give gifts—a practice which has become moreover a capitalist dream *tainted* with feelings of compassion. We also tend to respond generously in times of tragedy, such as natural disasters, when citizens of other countries have suddenly been made bereft of their essential needs. The United States as a nation makes significant contributions to humanitarian aid efforts throughout the world which are very admirable.

For the most part, our general populace is basically respectful and kind to each other. Overall, despite the draw of the news media, which hypes up the drama of any sort of shocking story, violence tends to be an aberration in the majority of our everyday interactions. And for many of us, there exists an overall atmosphere of tolerance and unspoken agreement to live together in a spirit of peaceful cooperation, however vague this may be.

Regardless, there is also an overwhelming and colossal amount of competition in our capitalistic society—which has very little to do with Christian values—wherein, making a buck and getting ahead of the pack are survival instincts that contribute to crushing our capacity for acts, let alone feelings, of compassion. From winning the game, to getting the girl, to landing the job, to scoring the business deal, we tend to live moreover in a spirit of competition than a spirit of interdependent and loving compassion.

It is only, perhaps, on Sunday morning, upon entering the church that our competitive streak is lessened and we allow our innate quality of compassion and spiritual community to come forth. Hence, for the majority of our lives we are moreover a Capitalist Nation than a Christian Nation. True Christianity, like any religion, is primarily concerned with the spirit; so how can we claim to be a Christian Nation when we are primarily obsessed with money and the competitive pursuit of materialist pleasures?

As Americans, we are raised to be weary of strangers, conditioned to protect ourselves from any perceived or imagined threat, and, above all, to "look out for number one" by advancing ourselves financially or socially whenever possible. The holy dictum "Love thy neighbor" has been degraded to "Suspect thy neighbor" because we've come to believe that no one can be trusted when it comes to our security and our belongings. Why else would we have locks on our doors, alarms on our cars, and passwords to our bank and email accounts? In the modern world, it has become almost unnatural to think of living any other way.

Did Jesus Christ advocate such a way of life?

The way of the isolated individual protecting his every possession and constantly working to become "better than others" by improving his social status?

No, he did not.

In fact, he spent the majority of his time with those who had naught. Yet this incongruity does not stop Christians or Americans from our selfish, materialist ways while simultaneously proclaiming ourselves to be devoted to a higher purpose or principle, to a God-figure that heralded love and spirit and suffering in the name of truth and liberation from the flesh.

Conversely to the life and teachings of Jesus Christ, in our American society we have chosen Capital over Christ, matter over spirit, self over other, safety over love, illusion over truth. But how many of us are willing to admit it?

In our modern world, we are constantly compared and contrasted with the performance of others, measured against the successes and failures of our fellows, all of which leads away from treating one another with Christ-like compassion and towards an atmosphere of interpersonal contempt. We are bombarded from all angles with messages that instill us with fear of one another, causing us to reclude into ourselves, to become overly self-protective of our belongings and our station in life, and to defend ourselves against any and all potential intruders upon the sanctity of our slice of the pie.

Most of us would agree that the opposite of love is fear, for where there is fear how can there also be love? Yet in almost every way our society, our media, and our way of life emphasize fear over love, thereby damaging our potential for living compassionately with one another.

When it comes to social problems which involve the suffering of individuals, families, and communities—such as homelessness, unemployment, the lack of healthcare or any failure to meet ones basic needs—we could improve upon the role that our current standards of compassion play in helping to ease one another's pain. Approximately 3.5 million people in America are homeless for a portion of every year, and every week about 842,000 Americans are homeless.

Of the total homeless population in America: 40% are families with children; 49% are African Americans, (who comprise 11% of the general population); 35% are Caucasians (who comprise 75% of the general population); 46% report chronic health conditions such as high blood pressure, diabetes, or cancer; 55% report having no health insurance (compared to 16% of the general population); 58% report having trouble getting enough food to eat; 54% were incarcerated at some point in their lives. Of this total number of homeless individuals, 72% experience a period of homelessness for over 4 months, and 20% for over 5 years.

These statistics portray large numbers of individuals suffering in ways that one would think could be averted in this *Land of Plenty*. But in a capitalist society, you can only get what you need if you have the cash, credit, or commerce needed to buy it. In a capitalist society, there will always be those who "fall through the cracks" into the marginal zones of day to day survival, struggle and strife. In reality, there is enough food, enough clothing, enough housing, and enough resources to go around; unfortunately our economic system encourages those who are "uber-wealthy" to horde these things while others go without.

Our economy is not based on compassion, but on competition. And the focus on competition generates greed, with success for some and failure for others. Some people work sixteen hours a day and are barely able to provide for their families, while others work half those hours but earn more money than they know what to do with—though they find ways to spend it on ostentatious extravagances.

In a society completely entrenched in capitalism, how can we consider ourselves to be a "Christian Nation?"

Globally, the United States ranks #1 in the total number of crimes committed with nearly 12 million crimes per year; #1 in assault crimes with about 2.25 million per year; and #5 in murders with over 16,000 murders per year—of course, this does not include the number of people we murder in the name of justifiable occupations and wars upon other countries.

According to these statistics, in comparison with the rest of the world, we don't appear to be employing any convincing examples of kindness to one another, be it "Christian kindness" or otherwise.

Insofar as we Americans live with an experiential relationship to a spiritual source, or are able to sacrifice our material, worldly endeavors for spiritual concerns, well, ahem ... these are, indeed, very rare qualities in the general populace. We seem, contra wise, to be increasingly disconnected from the spiritual side of life and much more caught up in exploits of technology and the material realms of our own making.

There is much, much more ego and self-centeredness in the typical American than one would believe was to be found in the figure of Jesus Christ.

If we were truly a Christian Nation, we would not be so nearly as obsessed with collecting personal items of material wealth as we are. I think it would probably be a better world if we truly were a Christian Nation, if we were truly "Christ-like," and if we did truly emulate and practice the teachings of Jesus Christ. However, in the final analysis, although some Americans proclaim the United States to be a Christian Nation, this is obviously moreover lip service and self-serving ego-enhancement than it is the truth. Either that or we truly aspire to be a more virtuous people than we are and just plainly fall very short of our intended goals.

BEFORE CONCLUDING this assessment of America's tendency to identify itself as a Christian Nation, I should state that I have been deeply affected by my own encounters with Christianity, mainly growing up as a child, then later as a young adult. At these times, Christianity was proposed to me in a coercive form, with the assertion that only through Christianity would I be able to go to heaven, and that, should I refuse to become a Christian, I would surely go to hell. Although, as an adult, this kind of high-pressure proselytizing approaches the ridiculous, as a child and young adult such "factual" and "authoritative" presentations were rather disturbing and disillusioning.

I later learned that the Christian faith involves a concept of original sin by which we are all *primordially guilty* for being humans; that, due to the actions of Adam and Eve, we are all "sinners" who must be saved by a "Saviour." Amongst all religions, this concept of original sin is unique to the Christian faith. I was never taken or convinced by the Christian belief system and the foundation of original sin upon which it rests, and so never, as an adult, have I considered myself to be a Christian.

As an adult, I learned that Christians, historically and often times as missionaries, have enforced their religion on the non-Christian peoples they encountered during the European colonization of the world—including Native Americans from Canada down through the United States, Mexico, and Central and South

America, as well as indigenous Africans, Australians, and East Indians.

Historically, Christian missionaries have been consumed with converting non-Christians, especially non-whites—who they initially referred to as "heathens"—to the Christian faith and a puritanical lifestyle.

This practice is utterly appalling to the non-Christian.

Why do fundamentalist Christians feel they need to convert others to their own unique belief systems and cultural values?

Why do they so often have such little tolerance for other people of other cultures who practice their own unique cultural ways and spiritual traditions?

This tendency of Christianity to force its religious beliefs and practices upon non-Christians is revolting.

That is, it provokes revolt because it subsumes the superiority of Christian thought over non-Christian thought, while denying other people of other cultures and other perspectives their own freedom of religion and uniqueness of identity. In short, Christianity, as other forms of fundamentalist religion, provides a mono-vision of reality which, to many folks, is merely an overly-myopic paradigm with socio-political undertones.

An essential aspect of any humanitarian value system is the allowance, respect, and support of the innate dignity of every human being. This innate dignity necessarily includes one's freedom of religion.

The fundamentalist—I should say extremist—Christian practice of converting non-Christians through coercive means is similar to the Western way of imperialism, in which we conquer other nations and enforce our way of life upon them so that we may benefit from their labor, resources, and materials.

This sort of thing is not merely a relic of the past—it still happens around the globe in third world countries where Christian missionaries are teamed up with lucrative corporations and big government.

However, there are many Christians who utilize their religion in a loving, kind, and respectful manner. I appreciate intentions and actions of this sort and believe that the true teachings of Jesus Christ did not include the unfortunate abominations which have been enacted throughout the centuries by many followers of the Christian faith.

In the United States, we are learning more and more about appreciating diversity, mainly due to the influx of many different cultures and ethnicities from the entire planet, not just Europe.

Appreciating and celebrating diversity is essential if we are to create anything resembling peace and harmony on this planet. Christianity is one religion among many, and people of all different religions would benefit from understanding each other because, as there are many different ways of living, many different traditions, and many different kinds of people, so there are also many different ways of approaching the divine.

XIV

STRANGERS IN A STRANGE LAND

T HESE DAYS, WHEN WE PASS a person on the street we usually don't say hello or even look them in the eye. In the city, we live in a world of strangers, the vast majority of whom we have very little to no personal relationship with whatsoever. Occasionally we may get into brief, interesting exchanges with the person behind the counter at the café or the grocery store, but these exchanges are predicated upon our purchase of something the shop is selling. This makes me wonder if such conversation is merely a byproduct of the capitalist machine in motion, a human byproduct of commerce whereby the exchange of cash sparks the expressive faculties while also providing an adequate social lubricant.

While it is, of course, natural for human beings to talk and communicate with one another, unless we have a good excuse or reason to do so we seem to maintain our typical everyday *stranger status* with the entire general public surrounding us.

I don't think we can underestimate the impact that living in a world of strangers has upon our psychological state of being. At times, I find it to be painfully awkward to continually encounter other people with whom I have absolutely no personal relationship. At these times, I almost always feel a sense of uncertainty. *Should I say hello? Or does it even matter?* The everyday atmosphere of a general lack of interest or caring between modern citizens can be overwhelming. But how can we care about other people who we don't even know when we live in a social context that supports a state of chronic alienation?

I know, I know ... you're thinking, "Well, but we're all supposed to develop our own group of friends, family, and acquaintances who meet our needs for human interaction, for fun, love, and affection." However, I must retort—notice how in talking about alienation I'm imagining *a relationship* of dialogue?!?—it doesn't always work that way. Statistics on depression and suicide demonstrate that meeting our own needs is an insufficient and tragedy-inducing agenda for a significant portion of all of us— over one million people commit suicide around the world every year.

Perhaps the assumption of complete self-care is just a preposterous joke based on the Western ideal of the heroic "rugged individual" who is ultimately responsible for meeting all of his own needs. As a citizen of the modern world, what does it mean, and *what does it feel like,* to be just one more human being lost in the crowd, in the midst of thousands of others?

Indeed, *the tribe*—an interconnected group of related individuals aspiring towards the mutual well-being of one another— has now become *the mob*—a collective of individuals who are, for the most part, unrelated and uninterested in one another, unless such interactions empower the individual to obtain their own financial, sexual, or social status-based objectives. I am not saying that tribal people were not selfish or self-interested, only that they appeared to have maintained an overall mutually reciprocal relationship with the larger community group in which they lived.

Although we boast of all the amazing benefits of modern living, there are many significant shortcomings in our having "evolved" from tribal to technological society, from a way of life centered around people, planet, and community to a way of life focused sharply on the individual and our ability to manipulate machines. Tribal societies function as a sort of unified whole, their members relying implicitly upon one another to meet their needs and fulfill their aspirations. Consider these words of the Pomo Indians of Northern California, from the book *The Way We Lived*, by Malcolm Margolin:

> What is a man? A man is nothing. Without family he is of less importance than that bug crossing the trail, of less importance than spit or dung ... A man must be with his family to amount to anything with us.

How does it affect us when the majority of others who we continually encounter are strangers? Perhaps this is why so many homeless or otherwise vagrant and lonely individuals are found talking to themselves or behaving as if they really are talking to another person who is not, objectively speaking, present. In a world of strangers, where few are ever interested in who you are, one may need to fantasize imaginary friends just to keep oneself company. Perhaps the insanity from which these people suffer is merely a psychosis born of the madness of alienation, the modern age insanity of strangers living in a strange land.

Like Morrison sang:

> People are strange when you're a stranger
> Faces look ugly when you're alone
> Women seem wicked when you're unwanted
> Streets are uneven when you're down

There is an ongoing sense of insecurity, an awkward, anxiety-pain associated with being in the world when we are alone and surrounded by strangers. The overall lack of emotional warmth or interest, the lack of familiarity and communication, and the lack of interpersonal relationship between people in public is truly bizarre. It's uncanny how rarely we ever comment upon this ongoing condition; like fish swimming in water we've become so acclimated to the sea of strangers surrounding us that we usually don't even notice it. This generally isolating influence of the modern world may be responsible for many of our shared woes, among them mental disease, depression, social disorder, suicide, crime, and homelessness.

How are we to resolve these problems in a world which does not promote communal harmony or intimate interactional engagement? Perhaps all these sicknesses are variations on the theme of homesickness, "home" being the original sense of familiar belonging, place, care, and love that many other cultures have nurtured for eons. Perhaps this sickness stems from our prevailing modern myth of the individual. However, to change our conceptions of selfhood from anything other than a primary focus on the individual is at absolute odds with the current thrust of capitalism.

AT TIMES, I FEEL SO INCREDIBLY sad, so profoundly alone in the midst of countless other uninterested, isolated individuals, as if we are all islands separated by the vast sea of loneliness. It incites a gash in my spirit, a rip in my being, a tear through my heart. In the general populace of the public, we are all so inconceivably disconnected from one another, so utterly alien—related only through the goings-on of commerce and survival—it is like an absurd existential joke.

Alone in the general public of modern Western society there is absolutely no hint of communal life, no genuine human contact or sharing. Indeed, our collective human condition has become a horrifyingly painful nightmare. The pressure placed on each individual in this society to carry their own weight and take care of themselves, in a virtual vacuum of truly intimate or communal humanity, is insane. In order to survive, most of us swallow the pain, don't talk about it, and make pretend it doesn't exist.

To admit that we feel pain would make us vulnerable to further attack or hurt. So we become trapped in a double-bind and must somehow cleverly work our way out of the situation while also finding a way to make ourselves feel better, to ease the pain, and furnish some kind of meaningful human connection. The modern world, for all its excess of activity and action, has become a painful and lonely place, a mechanical conundrum where services are provided and products exchanged between unrelated individuals—or, more recently, simply between humans and machines. Where is the heart or compassion in any of this?

The dark shadow of our claim to "Freedom in America" is the overwhelming isolation of the individual. Though we are continually told that we need to succeed on our own as individuals, in reality, succeeding alone is ultimately unsatisfying. And though politicians go on and on about the significance of the family, in truth, the very structure of our society splits the family apart, reducing each member down to the isolated part they play as individuals.

In essence, we are now a culture of individuals in pursuit of our own happiness. We don't feel the full impact of the family, the group, or the society anymore. We don't even really live in communities anymore, we live in municipalities, rapidly expanding conglomerations of social services and technological structures intended to feed narcissistic, solitary consumers.

As human beings, when we feel distant and unrelated to one another—through a lack of belonging, caring, familiarity or interrelationship—our normal capacity to function breaks down, we become psychologically, emotionally, and cognitively distressed. When our interpersonal needs are chronically unmet, we become upset, angry, and depressed. We act out against a world that has not provided what we need—either expressing our anger and discontent at this world that does not appear to care for us, or suffering our disconnection from others in near-suicidal silence and alienation.

Socially, we ignore or deny our loneliness and emotional deprivation out of shame, false pride, and fear of further humiliation or rejection. Collectively, as well, we ignore the causes of these painful problems that are built into the structure of our society.

Our general response is to treat depression medically with a pill that one can purchase. Isn't this amazing! While we suffer from a lack of meaningful human interaction and involvement, our socially sanctioned solution is also a capitalist solution, a consumer-based solution, a solution whose context and function are the same as those of the problem it portends to resolve—that of an impersonal, pseudo-relationship in which *a pill* is expected to address the ailments of the heart and soul.

Pills that alter our brain chemistry, pills that also impart new chemical imbalances—manifesting in "side-effects" such as sexual dysfunctions, insomnia, and constipation—cannot be the final solution to our social deficits and psychological problems. Sometimes pills can temporarily relieve problems that are deeply ingrained in the structures of our psyches, problems that are widespread, chronic, and culturally-induced, problems that also demonstrate our need to reevaluate our social structures and functioning, and alert us to significant shortcomings in our modern way of life.

But instead of looking more deeply into the source of our collective problems—an activity that could produce more long-lasting change—we seek the easy way out: a magical, medical "pill-solution," supported by psychiatrists, doctors, and, of course, the corporate pill-producing, pill-pushing backers of commercial media—a *solution* which is very rarely, if ever, a *resolution*. "Just take this little pill and *poof* all your problems will disappear!"

Perhaps the enormity of our collective, social and psychological problems are just too much for us to grapple. How can we admit that there are such tragic flaws in our basic functioning or in the makeup of our beloved social institutions; and, even if we do, how could we change these structures in ways that would recreate a world with less suffering and more compassion in action?

Perhaps all collective problems are just unavoidable, part and parcel of any imperfect human society, and we need to accept that we are an imperfect people who have manifested an imperfect world, and leave it at that. Perhaps our best course of action is to admit that we are merely human, that the best we can do is be honest with ourselves and with one another, let go of the denial of our mutual human suffering, accept it for what it is, and let the authentic encounter with suffering open our hearts to compassion for ourselves and the world.

For a world in pain, composed of a disjointed and confused people, perhaps the best answer is compassion. For when we suffer from a lack of relatedness—a lack of caring, belonging, love, and unity—compassion in action is what we need. How else will we heal or become whole? Therefore, we must learn to cultivate compassion for ourselves and, as improbable as it may seem, for the society of strangers in which we live.

We seem to be able to increase our communal compassion when we have a common enemy—as in times of war or natural disasters—through which we identify a common wound, a common threat, and a common goal. Is it possible to create a compassionate society through proactive, affirmative, and peaceful means, without the unifying bond of disasters or the polarizing catastrophe of war?

While the plausibility is questionable of creating a more compassionate society as long as we function under the rule of capitalism—in which competition is the key principle and motivating impetus—it is essential that we do. Although survival is an instinctual drive, and the will to power an ever-present force, compassion and lovingkindness for ourselves and the world of sentient beings are the evolutionary and conscious alternatives, and could become our prime priorities.

Early on in his illustrious career, the world's most innovative psychologist, C. G. Jung, perceived this when he wrote, "Where love rules, there is no will to power, and where power predominates, love is lacking. The one is the shadow of the other." In essence, for life to have meaning, and perhaps for life to continue at all, we must evolve our minds and our society to functional states based on compassion, on awareness of and concern for others, not just ourselves. For what meaning does a life of ego-aggrandizement and self-isolation carry? Whatever meaning it might glean is lethally limited by loneliness.

Perhaps when we're able to realize that as a human race and society we have become estranged from one another, when we're able to see this fragmented world for what it is, when we accept the pain of the world as our own pain and see our hearts in the hearts of others, when we're able to recognize that every one of us is essentially floating in the same boat, when we're able to walk down the street and feel our own footsteps resounding from other peoples feet, then, perhaps, we will begin to learn the value, the reality, and the necessity of compassion as the essential human capacity that will heal us from the temporary state of fragmentation into which we have fallen.

XV

WHAT HAPPENED TO THE *NATIVE* AMERICANS?

"There is no center any longer, and the sacred tree is dead."
~Black Elk, *Black Elk Speaks*

MOST CITIZENS OF THE MODERN United States of America are non-native, non-indigenous persons: immigrated, imported, implanted, and exogenous. Originally, the majority of us were of European ancestry, although now we are becoming an integrated mix of African, Asian, Pacific Islander, and Middle Eastern descent as well. Those who were originally of this land now occupied by our society we refer to as Native Americans, Mexicans, and Latinos. I've wondered why persons of native Mexican and Central and South American descent are called Latinos—this seems to be a prejudicial absorption of a huge chunk of their original identity into a neo–European identity, based on an ancient European language.

Although we are all now considered to be Americans, we of non-Native American descent did not originally rise up from this land; we came to it; our forefathers claimed it and stole it from those who were living upon it at the time.

Malcolm Margolin, a Native American historian and author, writes of the times when the land now known as California was first encroached upon by the invasive and racist conquest of white European pioneers:

> In 1769, when the first Spanish colonists arrived, an estimated 310,000 native people were living within the borders of the present state. Then came the missions and the *ranchos*; the goldminers, loggers and farmers; the silting of streams, clearing of forests, draining of marshes, fencing of grasslands, and elimination of game; the diseases, the hatred and the violence; the unspeakable tragedy. By the beginning of the twentieth century fewer than 20,000 native people were left in the state.

Although we habitually ignore the brutality and injustices of the past, of what nearly amounts to genocide, the truth is that the empire we've created was built by means of a criminal usurpation of lands, and a bloodthirsty eradication of peoples and cultures who did comparatively nothing wrong to deserve such horrific treatment. How ignorant and arrogant we must be to simply assume that our past transgressions are somehow magically "healed by time" or the passing of the wand from one generation to the next

Indeed, we don't like to think about this aspect of our history; we ignore it as if it amounted to some meaningless events that occurred in the distant past for which we have absolutely no responsibility or concern. We act as if it was completely natural for European cultures to have come here and have taken over, to have changed everything, to have constructed our massive, mechanical projects over top of all that had previously existed.

In fact, we've altered the world so radically that if you could transport a Native American person from 500 years ago to the present day, they would think they'd been brought to an entirely different place, an entirely altered earth, a crazy nightmare world. And yet we are so proud of all we have done, of all the marvelous changes we've inflicted upon the land, of all the beautiful mechanical creatures we've invented, the cars and roadways, the magnificent factories with all their miraculous technological devices and delivery systems, the construction of endless buildings and homes that we've erected across the horizon of what once was just a lonely planet inhabited by primitive savages. All the while, we ignore the industrial filth and pollution, the trash, the dumps, and the abandoned wreckage of machines littering the land.

We somehow believe that we've completely improved upon nature and the natural order through our tyranny of progress: through electricity, motor vehicles, mass-production of food and drink; through a billion forms of virtual entertainment and all that has come to fruition with our industrial-capitalist machine society that is based upon the acquisition of money and materials *at any cost.*

We glorify in the recognition that we have made everything so much easier and efficient; in the fact that we no longer must come face to face with the savage world of survival, with the beasts and vermin of nature; and in our attainment of power and control over all the unruly and unpleasant forces of nature which we view as threatening to our most lofty human stature.

Likewise, we exert the same power and control over our own kind, keeping our children fenced inside schools, and our fellow man locked up in the office and the factory, chained to the wheels of commerce as indentured robots in servitude to an unrelenting and systematic social machine.

We no longer serve nature or the spirit; rather, we serve the machine of society, the mechanisms of material profit and our own abstract ideals of worth, amounting to a heroic archetype of the imperialistic, triumphant man.

Indeed, we have "evolved" from the status of instinctively expressive hunters and gatherers enwhirled in a rich and ritualistic reality, to that of tame businessmen who crop their hair dangerously close to the scalp and all dress alike in the proper suit and tie format. The modern day hunter-warrior does not engage the natural world or the innate forces of the earth. No, today we battle the abstract, hierarchical powers and monetary structures of society.

We live less in the heart, in tune with our impulses, and more in the intellect, in line with conceptual reality. We operate not out of compassion and positive regard, but out of capitalistic principles of power and control—though we sometimes claim to be good negotiators.

Yes, the world which we have created and in which we live is a monstrous machine that we must constantly outwit. We must be painstakingly clever to optimize our opportunities and maximize our "growth potentials."

Our human nature is utterly manipulated and distorted through the grinding, mechanical demands of the system—the education system, the economic system, the employment system, the political system, the "justice" system, and the countless bureaucratic systems of "red tape"—and we now find it nearly impossible to be true to ourselves, or to feel truly alive without them.

BUT ENOUGH OF "US" and our current plight! What of the Native American who preceded us? Where are they now? Other than running gambling casinos for non-Native American tourists and ingrates to waste their time and money on distracting, meaningless, and superficial forms of entertainment? It doesn't seem as though we really care much about the genuine Native American cultural traditions or lifeways because they do not offer benefit or material profit to our own culture of capitalism, excepting in rare cases.

Although we've found it in our hearts to grant them a way of integrating into our modern capitalist schemes, via the gambling casinos, has this enabled them the opportunity to preserve and continue their own unique and traditional way of life?

Not really.

Of course, it's also true that they deserve a piece of the pie—the New World Order American Money Pie—just like the rest of us. Maybe after having been quarantined onto crappy reservation lands, completely marginalized and separated from our *White Man's culture* for so long—or having White Man's culture driven down their throats in a coerced conversion from their native ways to our own—they are now eager to become part of the new and radically developing world which we know as the 21st Century.

Why is mainstream America so hard pressed to acknowledge the cultural and spiritual realities of Native Americans?

Perhaps this should be obvious: because our way of life is so antithetical to native life, with our almost exclusive focus on the acquisition of money and materials at the expense of everything else. In all probability, it is also because we really don't understand the point of native life, or any perspective which tends to honor the earth or is concerned with attunement to nature, or claims to experience a spiritual reality embedded in the greater environment of the planet and universe.

Sure, we've had a few good, heartbreaking movies over the years about Native American culture and struggle—like *Dances With Wolves* and *Thunderheart*—but in the day to day world there seems to be almost no recognition that Native Americans are indeed Americans who live here in this country and who, in fact, have a very unique and historical perspective on this land and reality in general. In fact, it would appear to any given onlooker in our country like the Native Americans do not exist. Like they never did.

The truth is we are living in an inherited denial of the Native American's struggle to exist, alongside our having banished them from our favored cultural form of Christian Capitalism. Having segregated Native Americans out to reservations, we just ignore their presence, as if they didn't really belong to our country. Because it's far easier for us to live like this, remaining almost completely unconscious of the whole thing. It doesn't help that in grade school we're taught the idyllic version of Christopher Columbus having *discovered* America.

As children growing up in the White Man's world, we're not educated on the brutal truth of the European invasion of this entire American continent, which entailed the enslavement, cultural persecution, and death of millions of native peoples. Rather, through our primary education we are fed a false account of how our European ancestors came to occupy this land that was not their own to begin with.

To even say that we *discovered* this land is a Eurocentric illusion that completely dismisses the honest reality that hundreds of unique Native American tribes lived here for thousands of years before our arrival. In fact, according to Malcolm Margolin, Native Americans "first started appearing in California more than twelve thousand years ago."

The fact that we are still unjustly persecuting Native American people, and that they are obviously not accepted, valued, or well-integrated into the dominant society, can be seen in their unusually high incarceration rate.

According to The Foundation for National Progress, an umbrella organization of the magazine Mother Jones, "Despite being the smallest segment of the population, Native Americans have the second largest state prison incarceration rate in the nation." Their study found that Native Americans, including Alaska Natives, experienced an incarceration rate of 709 per 100,000 in 2000, second only to the incarceration rate of African-Americans at 1,815 per 100,000—both of which are ghastly, appalling, and indicative of the same kind of racism aimed at non-white ethnicities by the dominant culture.

In fact, Native Americans were not only decimated in this country we call the United States, they were also decimated down through the vast expanses of Mexico, Central America and South America, as well as northward throughout the land we know as Canada. Once again, Joe Kane provides a graphic depiction of the exploitation of Native South American lands and people by the United States:

> Since 1967 American oil development in the Oriente—as the Ecuadorian Amazon is known—had proceeded virtually without regulation. Every day the petroleum industry was dumping millions of gallons of untreated toxic pollutants into a watershed extending over fifty thousand square miles of rainforest, and it had opened the area up to such rapid and uncontrolled colonization that it was on a pace to be almost completely deforested early in the next century.

Kane refers to this contamination of native lands by American oil companies, which is second only to gold mining in Brazil, as "the worst case of toxic contamination in the entire Amazon." To put this in perspective, he states that Texaco "dumped into the Oriente more than one and a half times as much oil as the Exxon *Valdez* spilled off the coast of Alaska." The effects of such oil contamination of Amazonian lands has resulted in devastating consequences for its native inhabitants:

In 1993 a Harvard team of doctors, scientists and lawyers visited the Oriente and tested water from thirty-three sites. In particular, they tested for polycyclic aromatic hydrocarbons, or PAHs, an element of crude oil so toxic that the U.S. Environmental Protection Agency considers any amount at all to pose an exceptionally high risk of cancer. In drinking supplies the Harvard team found levels of PAHs up to a hundred times those legally permitted in the United States.

Drawing from research performed by Amazonian Activist Judith Kimerling, Kane states, "Malnutrition rates near oil-producing areas were as high as 98 percent." Additionally, in such areas, "Health workers reported exceptionally high rates of spontaneous abortion, neurological disorders, birth defects, and other problems linked to contaminants and predicted an epidemic of cancer."

It is especially disturbing when such heinous deeds enacted by modern Western society upon native peoples continue late into the 20th Century, into a time period past which we have witnessed equal rights movements for most previously subjugated and oppressed American citizens. It leaves me wondering when our wrongful persecution of Native American peoples will end.

American owned oil companies who have occupied and ruined areas of the Amazon such as the Oriente of Ecuador are only one example of how we now do our dirty work afar in a clandestine and devious manner, in third world countries such as those of Central and South America where the fallout of public outcry cannot easily reach us or the public eye.

Luckily, there are brave and brazen researchers, such as Joe Kane and Judith Kimerling, who venture down into these largely unknown lands and literally risk their lives to gather the facts that are kept conveniently hidden from most United States citizens and the rest of the world. In fact, Kimerling had to leave Ecuador due to death threats from persons tied to the oil company interests which she was contesting.

The typical modern American response to the claims of unjust occupation of native lands by mainly White persons of European descent goes something like: "Just get over it!" However, the increasing trend of diverse nations, ethnicities, and religions of humanity coming together to form global societies suggests that we could benefit from a conscious integration, a synthesis of native and modern cultures.

But before that can truly happen, the modern technological world must stop oppressing and destroying native cultures, which means ceasing exploitation of the Americas, the Amazon, and all lands where native peoples are still living—from Canada down through South America and around the world.

In the United States, there needs to be some kind of ongoing national acknowledgment of how things went down on these lands we now occupy. Once we openly and publicly own the fact of our past atrocities, at the least taking moral responsibility for the damages we have done, then perhaps a mutual respect can arise between the two disparate paradigms of native and modern culture.

Ideally, such a healing synthesis would also entail that traditional native cultural knowledge and learning styles be integrated, to some extent, into the modern education system. Because the modern world has succeeded so well in poisoning and destroying the planet, we need to learn from native cultures how to broaden our view of reality, which includes how we think about, experience, and relate to the planet.

❖

THROUGH THE PAST FIVE CENTURIES, there has been significant conflict and segregation between Europeans and Native Americans. Indeed, why would native people want to associate themselves with those who have conquered them, if only to survive in the aftermath? However, many of us living in the modern world realize that there needs to be some kind of healing between ourselves and those who originally occupied this land.

And yet, how are we to accomplish this in any meaningful way when so much damage has already been inflicted?

How can we reach out to those who have been devastated by our inherited culture?

Perhaps, we of the modern world need to develop some humility. Perhaps, we need to slow down the frantic pace of our lives to realize the world we've created—this material, ideological, and social world—is not the only option of living.

Through the current growing environmental crisis we are seeing the ill-effects of our disconnection from nature and our subjugation of the earth to our will. This realization is forcing us to change our way of life. But deeper than that, we have the opportunity to change our mind-set, our conscious, experiential relationship to the earth and to our bodies, as well as our relationship to native peoples, their traditions, concerns, and knowledge.

In this respect, we have much to learn from native cultures, and we should be willing to admit it. Indeed, perhaps changing our attitude from one of superiority and domination to one based on humility, respect, and genuine curiosity is the only available panacea for a technologically-driven culture which has devoured its own soul with an insatiable hunger for power and profit.

XVI

WHAT DO YOU DO?

ALMOST EVERY TIME I meet someone new at a party, they ask "So, what do you do?" By this, they are really asking "*What do you do to make money?*" They assume the way I engage capitalism is the primary feature of my identity: what *I do* is essential in determining *who I am*. Or perhaps it's just a socially safe question. But it always seems loaded, as if my answer can impart crucial information enabling the other person to size me up, to place me on a mental map defining where I reside in the structures of social status, or even worse, to think they have any kind of adequate understanding of who I am. (Not that I really have one either, but can't we at least make the reality of not knowing a little more fun?)

In reality, no one really gives a shit what you do. At least no one who asks you this question. They only ask the question to relieve themselves of the intolerable burden of anxiety they feel in the presence of a stranger. They also ask it because they lack the creativity to think of anything original. And you don't need more people like this in your life. So, the next time someone asks you what you do, just tell them you make people nervous. Then smile.

And walk away. (Disclaimer: This advice does not apply to job interviews with potential employers or conversations with lovers ...)

In order to provide instruction to the faint of tongue, the following is a list of introductory questions I would find far more engaging than the stale sockmouth redundancy currently under review:

Let's start with "So, where did you come from?" This question creates a point of reference, implying change and movement and continuum, and could be answered on a number of levels. I also like "What are you doing here?" It's honest and to the point. Or, how about "What's your story?" That's kind of exciting. Lastly, there's "What do you do for kicks?" We all like to talk about that, don't we? Seriously, I think I'd even prefer a blatant "Who the hell are you?!?" over the ever-blasé "What do you do?"

To be asked this same question, over and over again, this standard *question you ask a stranger at a party when you have nothing else to talk about* is just plain annoying. Wouldn't something unexpected and disorienting like "What *don't* you do!?!" be far more dazzling???

Who the hell wants to talk about *what they do* at a party anyway? I go to parties to escape, to forget about my wretched life, especially work, and hopefully lose myself in something or someone else. At least for a few hours.

When you really think about it, the question "What do you do?" is primarily concerned with how one fits in with the overall scheme of society, but some of us feel that *how we do not fit in* is more telling of who we are. I for one know that my identity has been more profoundly shaped by struggle, strife, and self-assertion against the odds than by how I conform to social expectations.

What I do for money seems secondary to what I do for meaning, for pleasure, for fulfillment, for soul survival, and for the sake of beauty. What we all do in the game of money often has very little to do with authentic self-expression because it rarely involves who we really are or our true creative spirit. And when I meet someone new, I like to think it's better to start off with how I define and experience myself, rather than how society and my attempts to engage the work system have defined who I am.

Don't you?

XVII

A PROBLEM TO BE SOLVED OR A MYSTERY TO BE EXPERIENCED?

"Certainly the ego and its will have a great part to play in life; but what the ego wills is subject in the highest degree to the interference, in ways of which the ego is usually unaware, of the autonomy and numinosity of archetypal processes."
~C. G. Jung, *Memories, Dreams, Reflections*

WE LIVE IN a de-mythologized world, a de-mystified, overly-enlightened, thoroughly sanitized and rationalized realm of reason, wherein everything can be mechanically measured, scientifically proven or disproven, and ultimately understood in terms of objective, factual evidence. Essentially, we've removed the *germ of life* from our version of reality—because it was too dirty, dangerous, and inscrutable to bother with. We experience life cerebrally and interpret life literally, *thinking our way through* the world each day. And we think everything has to make sense in a specific, pre-fashioned, previously understood, and prepared way. We're very uncomfortable with our bodies—with sensations, feelings, impulses, and urges—but we're the most discomforted by any kind of experience that involves *not knowing*—which, for us, translates as *not thinking* and, thereby, losing control—which is indeed only our illusion of control.

However, this new paradigm we inhabit is only another myth, a modern myth which, because we are living within it, enchanted, seduced, and sedated by it, appears to be *the true reality*. Although we project the status of myth onto other, "less evolved" cultures than our own, nonetheless, we live in our own myth, one which is based upon the worship of rationality, reason, logic, and total control as aspects of the new deity. Hence, there is little awareness or appreciation of mystery in the modern world because our societal myth portrays life as bereft of mysteries, as an explainable material and mechanical reality that science and reason have, or are gradually, summarizing through intellectual explanations.

How boring!

In our externally-focused, materially-constituted, and scientifically-based paradigm of reality, we view life as *a problem to be solved*, instead of *a mystery to be experienced*. This attitude conveys the atmosphere of our cultural need to remain in control, to live in the mind instead of the body, the head and not the heart, to place thinking above sensation and feeling, to value planning and scheming over *being* in the moment—linear, goal-oriented time over reflective, contemplative, experience-based, and *appreciative* modes of time—and the future over the present or the past. However, to allow yourself to *experience a mystery* implies letting go of control, trusting the unknown, and allowing yourself, your mind, emotions, and senses to be open and receptive, *thus in some way vulnerable*, to the influx of the world.

To experience a mystery opens up the possibility of being profoundly affected by forces beyond yourself and beyond your conscious control.

Opening yourself—your mind and heart, your awareness, even your spirit—to the world, to the unmitigated impact of the direct flow of life, requires some inner strength through trust in yourself and your own integrity. In truly opening yourself to the world, you may feel as though you are losing control, falling apart or psychologically breaking down, or you may experience a joyful and captivating transcendence of your limitations and boundaries, as in being completely fascinated and rapt by nature, art, or music, or even *falling in love.*

However, opening yourself to the world goes hand in hand with opening yourself to yourself; there are two worlds, or two sides to one world: the inner and the outer. Experiencing mystery begins with the mystery of who and what you are. Try to sit in a quiet room alone for half an hour, let go of thinking and see what happens ... To *know* yourself is not to *think* yourself; likewise the world is not primarily known through thought, but through experience. The problem is we've been taught otherwise our entire lives. Thus, for us, life has become a problem to be solved.

Our capacity to *experience a mystery* is the antithesis of our capacity to *solve a problem.* In our daily lives, we are more accustomed to solving problems, which requires sustained effort and will to *make something happen,* to manipulate and control something or someone outside of our own self; although in so doing we may also need to manipulate and control ourselves—our feelings, thoughts, desires, actions, inclinations, or needs. Just think about how you feel and function at work half the time—or all the time!

But how often, other than vicariously through Hollywood movies, are we truly encouraged to *open up to the mystery of life?* To allow ourselves to acknowledge the presence of a great unknown which forever dances just out of our reach, but which moves, inspires, and mystifies us just the same? To feel the immensity of silence and space that encompasses our busy lives? To engage directly with the powers of nature or with our own profound inner nature?

Most of the time we're instructed to "keep it together," "stay focused," "remain in control of the situation," "plan ahead," "be prepared," "stay strong," and to never reveal our weakness to the world. But these dictates only make us feel more anxious and insecure about living and represent an ideology that is contrary to who we are and how we naturally experience life.

In the modern myth which we inhabit we don't like to think of life or ourselves as a mystery. As a matter of fact, in modern Western society there are more laws and bylaws, guidelines, rules and regulations, and procedures and protocols to follow than ever before. There are stiffer penalties for not following these regulations, and more people per capita are imprisoned in the U.S. than in any other country for their failure to abide by them. We've become not only "one nation under surveillance," but a people moderated by an authoritative government that operates reactively and out of anxiety, suspicion, and control.

Living in such a context, motivated by social fears and anxieties—high unemployment, terrorist threats and wars based on lies, loss of civil liberties, and massive incarceration—in a paranoiac cultural atmosphere wherein we're struggling to survive, there can be little awareness or appreciation of mystery. The *powers that be* are now governmental and capitalistic—no longer gods and goddesses or other awe-inspiring nature deities—and merely figuring how to navigate through their minefield is simply exhausting.

And yet, we tout our society and culture as the most highly evolved and the most beneficial of any that have ever existed. However, on a daily basis we continue to look at life as a series or amalgamation of problems, while chronically failing to appreciate the aspects and dimensions of life that we do not institute, moderate, or control. Because our focus is so narrow and self-obsessed, we fail to appreciate the greater surrounding mystery, the cosmic reality, and the spiritual basis of life on earth which, in truth, exist according to powers far beyond our control or making, and, as such, deserve ample consideration and appreciation. Although solving problems is an important human function, I believe that our over-focus on this kind of mindset tends to eclipse our capacity for appreciating the mystery of life.

Perhaps we could learn to appreciate our problems without needing to solve them, for we will never "solve" life, so we might as well enjoy it.

XVIII

MONEY IS THE MEDIUM
OF THE MADNESS

"The hedonism of the West is the other face of desperation..."
~Octavio Paz, *Mexico and the United States*

IN A WORLD SATURATED with capitalist endeavors selling us the promise of continual self-improvement, it's no
wonder we've become a culture obsessed with perfection.
There are countless commercials and advertisements proclaiming
products for perfect skin, perfect taught bellies, perfect muscula-
ture, perfectly shaped bodies, perfect hair, perfect teeth, perfect
breath, perfect tits, and a perfect erection. If you've got the money, you can buy the *perfect* life—or so we're told.

Why are we so vulnerable, so impressionable to these images
and ideas of perfection? Why must we have a perfect complexion?
A perfect sex life? A perfect outfit for every occasion? A perfect
tan? A perfect attitude? A perfect car? A perfect job? A perfect
paycheck? A perfect personality? A perfect relationship? A perfect yada, yada, yada ... ?

As long as we're continually, obsessively striving for some ide-
alized state of perfection, we will forever be reminded that we are

not, and will never be, perfect. Why can't we accept our imperfections? Or recognize that we are, indeed, perfectly imperfect?

We need to learn to appreciate our imperfections as essential to our humanity, but you never see commercials about that because appreciating what you've got doesn't sell anything!

Why do we have such an immense ongoing dread of our flaws and shortcomings? Is it really that bad to be a little chubby or a little out of shape? Why can't we just be glad to be alive? Glad to be more or less healthy? Glad to be living in one of the most comfortable and entitled countries in the world? Why are we so incredibly vain and narcissistic about our image and our *performance*?

Why is it never enough to just be who we are? In the shape that we're already in? What's wrong with being a little sad or depressed sometimes? With not being utterly happy and completely satisfied all the time? What's wrong with being bored or lonely some nights? With being occasionally unproductive or feeling lost? What's wrong with having a bad day? Or going through periods of crisis—wherein we question who we are and what we're doing with our lives—without being instructed on having to take a pill that will magically make us forget all our troubles and feel better?!?

How has our society convinced us that we are inherently inferior and somehow *wrong* or *bad* if we suffer in any way, or encounter any element of imperfection in ourselves or our lives? How has society succeeded in making a mockery of our ordinary, fallible, perfectly imperfect human lives?

We feel the way we do because our persona-based society and the media keep us forever questioning ourselves and our worth on every level imaginable, conditioning and convincing us to feel the need to be perfect, to be always striving to improve ourselves and to out-do others.

And why do they do this?

Because it feeds them financially. And because it reinforces and justifies their capitalist reasons for being. The media and the salesman pretend that they can save us from ourselves, from whatever horrible affliction we must surely have, or will soon develop, if we don't abide by their necessary precautions which inevitably involve purchasing some remedy they must sell us. It's a very thorough process in which we're led to believe that we are helpless to help ourselves.

First, they demonstrate to us how imperfect we really are. Then, they admonish us that this is not okay. Lastly, they instruct us on how to be "successful" in all areas of our lives—as if we were worthless without their precious advice. Thus, we are summarily beguiled into believing that, in our current, natural state of being, we are inferior. Being compared to Hollywood stars or neurotic models in the media greatly enhances the effectiveness of this process.

Of course, being instructed on the right way to remedy ourselves invariably necessitates the purchase of some product or service that the capitalist salesman is selling.

In our fearful, conformist subservience to the collective voice, we're trained to become dependent on an outside authority— whether it's the doctor, the psychiatrist, the newscaster, or the car salesman—who will guide, shape, and mold our lives into the forms and formats that they dictatorially profess we should assume.

When we obsessively strive to improve ourselves and constantly question if everything we are and all that we do is good enough, then the life we are living is both fractured and fragmented. In this mode of being, we doubt and reject ourselves as we are, and our lives become games of running on the treadmill, of everaspiring to become acceptable in the cruel eyes of our own self-reproaching egos, and in the watchful and critical eyes of society at large.

Of course, the enterprising capitalist will prey on our vulnerability and our impressionability, as well as our self-doubt and lack of confidence—they profit from these negative, narcissistic, and neurotic traits which our society has implanted in us since birth.

In the capitalist regime we're constantly *sold* the idea that *we need more stuff to be okay*. When there are so many new products and services available to us, we feel like we always need more than we have, so we gradually learn to not appreciate what we already have to begin with. Indeed, we learn to not appreciate what we have because *our focus is on the process of obtaining new things,* not really on enjoying these things once we've acquired them. As we grow from childhood into adulthood, we're reared by the media into this way of being as it exercises a parental-like control over us which we obey to remain in good standing, so that we can continue to become *ever more successful* citizens.

Beyond their survival needs, pre-industrial, pre-Western cultures were more occupied with ritual activities, festivals and spiritual concerns; whereas we moderns occupy ourselves with relentlessly advertised consumer-based activities like going to the movies or shopping at the mall. Malidoma Somé, a medicine man and emissary of the Dagara people of Burkina Faso, West Africa, points to this contrast between modern and ancient cultures in his book *Ritual: Power, Healing & Community*:

> I am tempted to think that when the focus of everyday living displaces ritual in any given society, social decay begins to work from the inside out ... The fading and disappearance of ritual in modern culture is, from the viewpoint of the Dagara, expressed in several ways: the weakening of links with the spirit world, and general alienation of people from themselves and others.

Whereas the basis of traditional culture is involved in maintaining harmonious relationships with the spirit realm and the world of nature, the basis of our modern society is focused on maintaining monetary profits and material advancements through capitalism.

If our culture was depicted symbolically as a dining room table, the center piece would not be a bowl of fruit or a nourishing meal, a feather, tree, or animal, it would be the inedible and inanimate dollar bill, or perhaps a credit card—thus demonstrating the absurd reality of our preoccupation not with life itself, but with an abstract symbol of power, which, in and of itself, is basically meaningless and useless. Our obsession with it, therefore, is undeniably ridiculous.

If one possesses money, one can acquire many of the tangible things one wants or needs, but not the more intangible things, such as happiness, love, authentic friendships, and creative fulfillment. Spiritual things, like an understanding or relationship with God or an alignment with one's greater purpose in life, cannot be bought either. Money is a human creation that only works in the social systems we have devised.

In and of itself, *materially speaking,* money is just colored paper and virtually worthless. Money means nothing to animals or other forms of life on this planet and would mean little to us without the specific human overlay of value which we place upon it.

Ironically, because money is our collective symbol of worth, we grow to value money more than the actual things that money provides for us.

The use of money as the medium of power, energy, and value in our society acts to distance us from the actual things in life which keep us alive physically, emotionally, creatively, and spiritually—things such as food, clothing, music, and books. Money triangulates us with the things we buy; making us passive third party participants to the actual products and services that we need, or even want, to live.

LET'S THINK THIS THROUGH in practical terms. The main areas of expense on which most of us spend the bulk of our money are: 1) housing; 2) food and drink; 3) transportation; 4) health care—both physical and mental/emotional (for those of us who have access to health care); 5) heat, light, and electricity; 6) clothing; 7) communication—phone, internet, mail; 8) entertainment, study, and travel. Of course, there are others, but this is a basic list of our most common expenditures in modern life.

In the modern world, the vast majority of us work a job for which we are paid a specific pre-arranged and agreed upon amount of money. Our job usually does not entail that we directly procure or produce any of the above listed *necessities*—especially for our own sustenance—which are essential aspects of our modern survival and lifestyle. For instance, very few of us build our own homes, grow our own food, or make our own clothing.

To procure these items we must engage a third thing, "a job," whereby, through devoting half of our entire waking hours, or more, to tasks that usually benefit our boss or mammoth corporations more than us, we are paid an abstract medium called money—green colored paper, or what Lame Deer calls "green frog skins"—with which we then purchase the things we need to survive, or the things we *must have* to be an active, engaged, and thriving member of society—things like a brand new Porsche, a diamond necklace, or the latest iPod.

Ironically, most jobs grant no direct experience or training with obtaining the things we actually need to live, as noted in the list above. Most of us have no idea how to survive outside of the construct of modern society—if the economic system broke down completely and we could no longer *purchase our survival,* we'd be dead meat. In striking contrast, members of indigenous cultures through-out the world are methodically taught how to interact with the living, ecological environment and how to maintain harmonious relationships with the spirit world because both of these are essential to their survival and well-being.

Within indigenous cultures of Ecuador, "by the time he is ten a Huao [a member of the Huaorani tribe] is expected to survive on his own." Can you imagine a citizen of the modern world surviving on his or her own at age 10?

Not likely.

Some jobs feel like a natural exchange of our efforts for our pay, and involve our own unique energy, talents, and purpose on a deeper level for good in the world. Nonetheless, our jobs still distance us from direct involvement with the actual things we need to survive. Our jobs, like the rest of our lives, tend to separate us from the earth and preclude us from learning or understanding anything about our terrestrial purpose or function as organic and spiritual beings on this sensuous planet.

Working all day in an office or factory—our bodies and souls cut off from their source as we're shut off from the natural world inside a box—does not feel like the way we were meant to live. Does any other creature on the planet live like this? Ants inside their hills and bees inside their hives come to mind; however, ants and bees spend much of the day moving deliberately and productively throughout the natural world.

In reality, we are owned by our jobs. When we're working our time is not our own and, in many cases, when we're working it feels as if our lives don't even belong to us. Many jobs require activities and role-playing—for instance, customer service, sales, and hard labor jobs—that involve a severe manipulation of our personalities, our bodies, or our physical capacities. Many of us can't even be honest at work, we can't relax, and we have to repress our true impulses.

When we're done working, we feel psychologically or physically maimed. We have to do something to recover like smoke cigarettes, drink alcohol, do drugs, or overeat unhealthy foods. Many of us just zone out on the TV for hours after work because we feel depleted or even defeated by our jobs.

The severity of some jobs crushes our spirits. Sometimes it robs us of our very lives—in the U.S. alone 13 million people are injured on the job every year resulting in 70,000 work-related deaths. After work, just getting home through traffic and feeding ourselves is about all we can manage. We're thrilled when the weekend comes, but it's always too short, and on Sunday nights we dread returning to the work week ...

Yeah, you get the point: for most of us, WORK SUCKS!

It's nearly impossible to escape our jobs, or the debilitating impact that they have upon us, because we live in a capitalist society based on the acquisition and exchange of money for the goods and services we need to live. And because we're dependent on this system, we rarely obtain the occasion to question it.

Nonetheless, many of us feel trapped by our jobs, and we dread going to work. We fantasize about getting rich and play the lottery hoping to draw the winning ticket. Hoping to hit the jackpot, we think, "Oh, what I'd do if I just had the money!"

Ironically, many of the instant millionaire lottery winners end up with severe psychological problems, not very happy at all. If only we just knew how to survive on our own, then we wouldn't have to keep working for the boss, the company, or the capitalist scheme. But why would our education system teach us that? Then we might just break out of the system!

❖

PERHAPS HAVING OR NOT HAVING lots of money does not make the real difference in life. Perhaps what makes the real difference in life is in finding a way to live, a vocation that affirms our innate human qualities, that grants us a true sense of purpose, enjoyment, and fulfillment of meaningful goals. It is no easy feat to retain and develop your own essential humanity living in a world that revolves around money, a world that is moderated and manipulated by money. Although money rules our world as the centerpoint of most social interactions—as the crux of societal activity—the source of inspiration for our human lives is, in truth, our hearts and imaginations, our relationships, and our deeper callings.

In our own way, each of us must resolve the tensions and contradictions between the social emphasis on money and our own inner human need to live with meaning and purpose, to live with a sense of *heart* and with connection to our emotions and our souls. It is ironic that men, who are the traditional money-makers in our society, suffer from a much higher rate of heart disease and heart attacks than do women. This sad fact points to the state of estrangement that men tend to feel with their innermost being.

Hopefully, as our society progresses, we will realize a better balance between our valuation of money and our focus upon our hearts, between concerns with our outward success or material achievement and our true inner beings. Perhaps, ultimately, some kind of true integration of the two will occur. Currently, however, we're overly-preoccupied with the material world and the abstract medium of money.

It's easy to lose touch with our hearts in a world that revolves around money—a substance that, in essence, represents the power to participate as one wishes in this capitalist's dream. Men in particular are taught and conditioned to earn as much money as possible because for a man to become *truly successful* he must become rich with power. Men are taught that money is the magnet with which they will attract *the good things in life:* friends, lovers, attention, admiration and affection, a stylish car, a luxurious home, and an assortment of other material goods aimed to increase his security, pleasure, and social status.

Yes, modern man is trained to be a hedonist. Men especially come to believe that they need money and power to acquire love and sex. Money becomes a man's primary concern because it potentially opens the door for him to find a human relationship that feeds his heart. However, often times, a man tends to focus his energy on acquiring money and power to the detriment of his heart and to the detriment of his closest, most important relationships with his friends and family.

At some point, a person may have to choose between money and love, between the power to manipulate the world for a material profit, and the potential of seeking one's true mission and fulfillment based on goals and desires that are essential to one's integrity and authentic sense of self. A few of us find that we can do both, that by acting in accord with our inner truth, pursuing our own dreams and visions, the money comes. Look at people like John Lennon, Bono, and others who have creatively expressed themselves with a tremendous sense of heart, concern, and compassion for the world.

However, the basic formula that most of us follow, especially men—*that money can buy you love, and everything else you need*—is a very dangerous and destructive motto by which to live. When profit becomes the main concern, our values and ethics tend to disintegrate. In this way, money—the way we use it and conceive of it—works in opposition to our being human by enabling us to disregard and hurt other people, as well as the planet.

Unfortunately, almost everyone is drawn by the allure of money, as it exerts an insatiable seduction of otherworldly power upon us with the potential to contort us into obsequious, fawning sycophants like the little monster Sméagol in *The Lord of the*

Rings. It seems we will do almost anything for money. As kids, many of us reveled in playing the outlandish game of "*What would you do for a million dollars?*" in which we conjured up the most disgusting or outrageous, forbidden or taboo things we would do. Even adults on TV shows like *Fear Factor* are tempted to enter into all kinds of revolting situations to get a hefty wad of cash—which is a direct reflection of the magical qualities with which we have imbued money.

I'm sure we won't get rid of money anytime soon, or the principles of abstract value, worth, and wealth that it conveys. However, we would benefit by becoming more aware of how money impacts us and our relationships with the world. Money obviously creates massive divisions between people as it generates *classes* of rich and poor, the *haves* and the *have nots.* Or as George W. Bush put it, "*The haves* and the *have mores.*" Those who have lots of money tend to not want to associate with those who have very little—they like to stick with other rich folks. When they're driving through poor neighborhoods they roll up the windows, lock the doors, crank up the a/c and the car stereo, and stare straight ahead.

The affluent class, the "middle class," and the impoverished class are all in-groups, subcultures based on having or not having money, believing that, as a direct result of their lack or abundance of cash, they share such significant traits that they're better off sticking together. This kind of attitude is called classism and is just another kind of "ism," as equally destructive as racism or sexism—though we rarely acknowledge it.

Often times, the rich and the poor despise each other, they pre-judge and blame each other for social problems that have become the source of their own class-specific woes. The poor despise the rich for having what they don't have and for *keeping them down*; the rich despise the poor for *being* poor, for burdening the economy by being dependent on social services and using up too much of their taxpayer dollars. The poor man sees the rich man as selfish and arrogant, while the rich man sees the poor man as lazy and pitiful, maybe even dumb.

The main problem created through classism becomes an obfuscation of our shared humanity, as each member of a particular class sees, describes, and defines members of the other class through the lens of materialism and money, not through the lens of an open mind or heart, and, thereby, fails to perceive and appreciate the true qualities of the other person or group of people. Through the eyes of classism, we project our own denigrating, negative ideas and images or our own idealizing, positive ideas and images of the other class onto the particular person, thereby eclipsing our ability to truly see the individual person who, in reality, transcends the general profile of the class in which they reside.

This is another way that money dehumanizes, even *demonizes*, human beings. Of course, it is not specifically money, but how we relate to money, how we define it, and the power that we've placed upon it that enables us to distortedly judge one another according to how much money we each earn or possess.

Like sex and race, we're born into our class; although, through our own efforts or the twists and turns of fate, some of us are able to change this later down the road as adults. Maybe this is why classism can be even more pernicious than other kinds of "isms," because the person is resented for having actually succumbed to their class by means of choice.

The lyrics from the song *Wish You Were Here,* written by Roger Waters and David Gilmore of the psychedelic rock band Pink Floyd, portray the effects of living in a materialistic society that eclipses the soul. They remind us that what is really worth living for is not the *things* we have in life, but *how* we live, and with *who* we share our precious moments:

So, so you think you can tell
heaven from Hell,
blue skies from pain.
Can you tell a green field
from a cold steel rail?
A smile from a veil?
Do you think you can tell?

And did they get you to trade
your heroes for ghosts?
Hot ashes for trees?
Hot air for the cool breeze?
Cold comfort for change?
And did you exchange
a walk on part in the war
for a lead role in a cage?

How I wish, how I wish you were here.
We're just two lost souls
swimming in a fish bowl,
year after year.
Running over the same old ground,
what have we found?
The same old fears.
Wish you were here.

ONE WAY TO CHECK YOURSELF to see if and how far your
life has strayed from your heart is to ask yourself, "What would I
do—with my life, my energy, and my time—if money was not an
issue?" This question is not suggested for purposes of self-
recrimination, but as a potential way to become more aware of

what is important and meaningful to you. Nor is it intended to be a naive suggestion that we should all quit our jobs and do only as we please, although that does sound nice!

We all need to survive, and we each have our responsibilities which, for some of us, include supporting our children and families. In this world, all of that usually requires earning money. Although life is obviously not about just doing what we want, becoming more aware of what we really do want, other than money, and taking active steps towards incorporating that awareness into our everyday life can be immensely helpful. Outside of all our monetary commitments, we also have a responsibility to ourselves, to our inner experience, to that which *calls* to us, and to this one life we have as the unique person that we are.

So then, *what would you do if you didn't have to make money?*

If you didn't have to spend the majority of your waking hours at a job? Think about it, and write it down. Imagine what you would do, where you would go, who you would be with, what you would want to explore, experience, or accomplish. Perhaps you feel as if you came into this life to fulfill a particular purpose that is gradually revealing itself to you through your intuitions, visions, development, and desires, and perhaps there are ways that you can pursue this purpose without the necessity of money and a job being such a burden.

Your heart and spirit appreciate when you listen to them; the more you listen, the more they talk. And the more you put their voices and instructions into action in the world, the more the world will respond, opening new paths for to you explore that you never knew existed. But it all starts with listening to your inner voices, your intuitions, your inner awakenings, dreams, desires, and visions.

Knowing who you truly are, from the inside out—aside from the expectations that society and family have of you—is of vital importance. This idea goes back to the ancient Socratic instruction, "Know thyself." Developing awareness of your inner self is even more important in our modern society, wherein power and materialism are far more emphasized than deep feeling, love, integrity, generosity, creativity, and imagination.

Those who control our world, our economy, our politics, and our way of life do not seem to advocate spiritually or psychologically enlightening pursuits, because their baseline is their bank accounts, their material conquests and social status. Our society is governed by an Apollonian archetype—the solar, omnipotent ideal of masculine logic and power—as visualized by the eagle flying across the face of the sun. When taken to a one-sided extreme, the Logos principle that rules our world lacks feeling, empathy, depth, tenderness, and care. We were not made to live our lives exclusively as warriors.

As Moore & Gillette describe so well in their books on masculine archetypes, we have to balance our capacity to *act as warriors* with our capacity to *feel as lovers*. As an archetypal or universal energy or way of being, they state "The lover remembers the original unity of the psyche, and throughout the course of our lives, drives us toward recovery of that unity in complex form." The archetypal lover—much like the ancient, indigenous healing archetype of the shaman—is concerned with achieving states of unity within oneself and with the world. But the spiritually and sensuously stultifying conditions of modern life have blocked the lover's drives towards unity:

> A dark and chthonic Eros, split off and repressed by a society of workaholics, has returned to our broken world with a vengeance. The stockpiles of nuclear weapons and the effects of massive pollution are testimony to the rage of denied Eros.

Moore & Gillette define Eros as do I, not in its commonly understood context of *erotic desire*, but primarily as "the yearning of the human soul for union with the Divine." In our culture, we are often denied fulfillment of our need for unity—for relationship, love, and connection—and have overly-compensated for this lack of belonging by focusing our energies on separatist modes of action, inclined towards individual accomplishments, and on technologies that emphasize the communication of information, not the sharing of feeling or emotional warmth.

Another factor of modern society that impedes our drives toward unity of any kind is that of transience, in which we are always moving from one place to another, one job to the next, one girlfriend/boyfriend/husband/wife to another, such that it sometimes becomes impossible to lay down roots and for those roots to grow and to be nourished. As previously stated, we live— almost to the fullest extent possible—in the *Myth of the Individual,* wherein *I do* whatever *I want; I accomplish* whatever *I can*; and *I become* whoever *I want* to become, all on our own self-defined terms. As modern citizens of a "brave new world," we don't like to be *tied down,* or *hung up* on anything that limits our freedom—yet many of us are rootless and ungrounded, lacking a solid sense of belonging.

Although we're increasingly free to roam about as we please, to travel, to move, and interact with others as we wish, something else—our capacity or, perhaps, our inclination to experience deeply satisfying and long-lasting attachments with others—has shrunken. In times past, our communal needs for belonging, for unity and identification with a living group, tribe, or family were fed through the roots of our family or tribal tree, through which we drank in nourishment from deep, deep down below our individuality, inside the matrix of the universal human mystery that transcended, and made possible, our individual being and meaning.

Nowadays, however, we all seem to live far *above ground*, in the glorious light of individual consciousness and "image-reality," where it is assumed that the individual person is his own greater meaning and purpose—we've lost our roots, and with them we've also lost our depths and our connection with universal streams of being and identification. We live too much in the free air of our conceptual individuality and too little on the solid ground of our universal, family, or tribal being. In our aspirations to reach the stars we have certainly become more free; however, our freedom has come with a miserably alienating side-effect.

We've lost touch with where we came from, and—since virtually no one in this modern society truly knows who he or she is because technology has broken the organic spiritual connection—most of us float around "untouched," uncommitted, unrelated to one another and moreover like observers of life. In essence, we've lost touch with the soil of our origins and the soul of our humanity.

IN THIS RAMPANT *Age of Information*, the mystery of *being* has been extinguished. Ironically, our frenzied pursuits of information, of *in-forming* ourselves, of filling in the forms of our minds and bodies and lives and whatever we are, is based on a relentless and aching inner anxiety and emptiness. Through relying so exclusively on the externally-focused, stimulation-based realm of technology we've eclipsed some deeper dimension of our inner selves, our unconscious half, our unseen inner soul, as if by pretending it didn't exist it would cease to be or just go away.

Many of us have little time for deep feeling, connection, or reflection as we wander alone and heroic in this society of liberated hungry ghosts and make-up artists. We're usually too busy trying to make a buck or hustle the system to consider authentic expression and contact with the world—because we've been told that's not what the world wants.

The development of our own society-approved agendas towers over our consideration of true community with others, or even with ourselves. The *Age of Information* is also the *Age of the Individual*, in which each person has been reduced to all the gatherable facts that can be assigned to her or him by objective scrutiny. In the *Age of the Individual,* not only do we carry our loads alone, we also carry lonely loads, because the *Age of Information* has transfixed our identities from our original body-soul matrix to only those characteristics that can be categorized and dealt with through the new bureaucracies of the overly mentalized mind.

The pain of loneliness and isolation—not only from one another, but from who we essentially are—is the unacknowledged underside of our modern liberation from the tribal group. Our lives lack depth and consist of mainly superficial occupations, as the distance we experience from the center of our own souls manifests in the distance we experience from other beings and their souls. Thus, the *Age of Information* has succeeded by *in-forming* our interior situation with abstract data, news, "education," and meaningless entertainment, such that we have begun to mirror the exterior situation of technological society, which, of course, society has executed upon us in order to perpetuate itself.

THE LAND UPON WHICH we were born and with which we grew up is also a part of who we are and is akin to our ancestors; when we leave this land, this place, we also leave a part of ourselves. In a new land, a new place, a new city or town, we are not only surrounded by new people but also by "new history," by unseen moments and memories that do not belong to us. So we get a perspective on our life that is moreover the contrast of differences around us, which reinforces our own sense of separate individuality. This new perspective may serve to challenge us to grow in new ways, but it does not encourage our deeper sense of belonging to, and being a portion of, the world around us.

Here in the United States, we've built our empire on the desecrated remains of Native American Indians, whose extermination by us may likely haunt us until we make greater efforts to resolve our wrong-doings and make peace with our past actions against them, if that is even possible. This land was not the land of our ancestors, though, of course, with every succeeding generation it is becoming so. Therefore, in the United States, it could be postulated that we are in essence a people cut off from our past, cut off from our inherited history and the familiar spirits who would inhabit the land of our forefathers. No wonder we live as if we are half-crazy!

THERE IS AN INHERENT PROBLEM with capitalism when you need a job to survive, but there are more people than jobs so we can't all find a job; therefore, we can't all survive!
Most of us are born into our lives within towns or cities where survival is contingent upon possessing money and partaking of the mainstream economic system—very few of us live in areas where we would have the option to grow, hunt, or raise our own food, the capacity to procure our own shelter, and the ability to live self-sufficiently with nature. These days, most of us live in concrete jungles where we've got to survive in social systems, dependent on the job market and a capitalist world wherein the goal is monetary profit.

We don't play by nature's rules anymore, but by man's, whereby our instincts are divorced from their earthly origins and we must learn how to adapt to the materialist game of money and machines—we've got to learn how to operate cash registers, computers, coffee makers, and cars instead of how to navigate earthy terrains and interact with biological plants and creatures. In the modern world, our ability to manipulate machines and the marketplace maintains a close connection with our ability to make money, and, thus, to survive—although, this also succinctly involves the manipulation of other people and nature itself. It's still a survival of the fittest, only in a mostly manmade, industrial, world.

Perhaps the whole premise of modern technological society is infused with beliefs and behaviors that are antithetical to the life of the spirit and the innate dignity of human beings, in which the soul's survival is threatened. Along these lines of thought, Malidoma Somé writes:

> Western culture derives its power from machines or machine-like processes that are part of a Machine culture ... I am suggesting that Machine culture is a violent break away from the realm of spirit ... Western machine technology is the spirit of death made to look like life. It makes life seem easier, comfortable, cozy, but the price we pay includes the dehumanization of the self ...

Even our relationship to time is all-consuming and has entranced us into a hypnotic daze of mechanically regulated schedules in corporate rhythms—from school to work to death—abolishing our capacity for seeing outside of our systemized programming. Malidoma continues:

> The clock tells you everything and keeps you busy enough to forget that there could be another way of living your life. It has made the natural way of living look primitive, full of famine, disease, ignorance and poverty so that we

can appreciate our enslavement to the Machine and, further, make those who are not enslaved by it feel sorry for themselves.

The matrix of the machine world of industry, technology, capitalism, money, and materialism into which we are born governs almost every aspect of our entire lives. The true nature of this matrix is not spiritual or generative, but is based on profit at any cost through manipulation of people's lives, as well as the wanton destruction of the earth. This is why Malidoma says that modern life is at odds with the heart of the earth and humanity.

Of course, he has lived in a cultural reality so distinct and different from ours that, from our own point of view, his assertions may appear to have no grounding. According to Malidoma, this only goes to show how far modern life has strayed from ancient, tribal society and lifestyle:

> The Machine has made itself look beautiful by making other ways of life that have existed for tens of thousands of years look silly, shameful and uncivilized. But the truth is that the Machine must eliminate every alternative to itself and focus every attention on itself because it knows that its purpose is not to give life, but to suck the energy out of it. *We have therefore come to the point where it is not possible to think of life outside of the context created by the Machine...*

The way in which modern culture portends to be leading and guiding the entire world into the future is in synch with its underlying assumption that it is the only true and correct option which all humans have to abide by. Yet, as we see continued ecological destruction, rising crime and incarceration rates, and collapsing world economies, we begin to get an inkling that perhaps the grandeur and self-inflatedness of the modern world may bring about its own demise.

At some point, we will indeed evolve beyond capitalism with its "every man for himself" motto, as well as beyond technology and machine-based industry which holds as its central moral thesis that modern human culture may continue to develop itself infinitely at the expense of the other cultures, the other animals and the entire natural world.

From his experience with indigenous life in the village of Burkina Faso, Africa, Malidoma distinguishes between modern and tribal society:

> Thus the two worlds of the traditional and the industrial are diametrically opposed. The indigenous world, in trying to emulate Nature, espouses a walk with life, a slow, quiet day-to-day kind of existence. The modern world, on the other hand, steams through life like a locomotive controlled by a certain sense of careless waste and destruction. Such life eats at the psyche and moves its victims faster and faster along, as they are progressively emptied out of their spiritual and psychic fuel.

The question raised is how do people living in a machine and industry-based, materialistic world retain any kind of living connection with the spiritual side of life and with their own innermost soul or essential nature?

Can we truly experience or maintain a connection with God, the divine, or our own spirituality when we're choking on exhaust fumes in traffic, late for work, battling anxiety with road rage, surrounded by strident horns and sirens and recklessly impatient drivers? Or when we have been fired and can't pay the rent? Or when we're seriously sick and don't have the money to see a doctor?

Can spiritual reality be found in a man-made world? Perhaps if the men and women who created this world did so with a recognition of their relationship with spiritual dimensions, but this certainly is not the case inside the box-culture of offices, banks, factories, and billboards. Are we willing to admit to ourselves that we have, indeed, become alienated from some deeper sense of connection with the planet, each other, and the mysterious life-force that is responsible for our very existence? Or will we continue on our ego-centered paths of myopic fixation, promulgating the aggrandizement of modern society?

Malidoma goes on to state:

> Any person in modern culture who is aware of this destruction from the machine world upon the spiritual world of the individual realizes that there is a starvation of the soul. To be in a machine-like culture is to have one's soul constantly at risk of being sucked out.

In some sense, we've already had our souls sucked out and are frantically searching for something to fill in the space of our inner emptiness. Look around you and see that capitalism is at the ready to sell you anything that might fill the hole, just as long as material profit can be gained from such a transaction. In the modern world, we live in a pervasive catch-22 situation: although we have extensive access to many of the finest accoutrements and conditions of living—which contribute immensely to our comfort, safety, well-being, and entertainment—it all revolves around money, for which we must willingly sacrifice everything—our time, our energy, and our very souls.

So then, who are we? What have the consequences of such a contradictory arrangement inflicted upon us? What have they made us into? Do we even know?

REGARDLESS OF THE MECHANISTIC systems by which we are governed, I believe that most people put forth their best effort to survive, to sustain their lives and the lives of their families, while also contributing to the greater good of the community, or country, as they are able or inspired. But the process is confusing these days because individual survival has become so distinct from the survival of the community. There are so many of us that our own personal roles in the greater community, the town or city, may seem blurry, unimportant, and uncertain.

With so many people, we realize—whether consciously or not—that the town in which we live *doesn't really need us* to survive. Living in such impersonal circumstances, we may simply feel lost in the swarming masses. Someone working as a clerk at Home Depot, a cashier at Burger King, or even a computer programmer at IBM, knows that they are dispensable because just about anyone can do their job, and there is probably already a large stack of applicants in the manager's desk drawer waiting to be reviewed and called upon.

Because we live in such highly populated, impersonalized cities, it seems most of us lack significance or unique value in the eyes of our community. So if we aren't really needed by the group in which we live, what keeps us connected to that group, if nothing more than the need to survive and make money? And if we are not really valued by the community, do we learn, in turn, to not value the community?

Increasingly, it appears that *the nucleus of modern society is the individual,* not the family. But how does the individual place him or herself into the greater whole as a significant and valued member of the community other than in purely material terms of elevated upper class status achieved through the cunning contortions of capitalism?

Remember, the root of the word *community* is *unity.* The word *community* almost breaks down to the two words *common unity,* or even, *communal unity*—God forbid we realize that it is also ever so close to the word *communism,* just two letters away! Although we like to think of ourselves as living in communities— the word *community* is really such a heartwarming word—with so many people walking around in our towns and cities, so many people virtually ignoring each other every day; can we really continue to call what we live in a *community?*

If so, just what is our community, our "common unity," or the unity we all share in common?

Is it simply based on a collective striving to meet our basic human needs and desires, those which the psychologists have so neatly broken down and articulated?

Or do we all truly share a common vision?

Are we all living *The American Dream?*

If so, just what does this mean? Are we all dreaming the same dream? Or are there many different dreams being dreamt under an illusion of a common dream?

What exactly is The American Dream?

Freedom, justice, and liberty for all?

What does that really mean in a society where the unemployment rate is 10%; there are 2.5 million citizens locked inside the cement tombs of jails and prisons; thousands are homeless, hungry, and malnourished; and thousands are sick or dying because they are in need of health care that they cannot afford to procure for themselves and which our *community* does not provide for them?

If we lack a unifying commonality, a shared vision and purpose, then perhaps we should just admit it, just say we're all in it for ourselves and call it a day—isn't this what the *free market enterprise* of capitalism, our new religion, is all about anyway? Can't we at least be honest with each other?

Understandably, this is made more difficult because our elected politicians and government officials are continually lying to us. Selfishness and greed are not typically considered to be ethics, but I think we could accept them more easily than flat-out dishonesty and deception.

We sometimes see painful, difficult, and disturbing expressions of honesty in the arts, in music, literature, film and poetry; so why do we so very rarely see it in politics and business? Because the main motive of business and politics is to manipulate the masses for the ultimate goal of self-serving material benefit, which requires maintaining power and control over us, whereas the arts are more concerned about reckoning with us in an attempt at an authentic relationship—although self-serving material motives may also be at play here as well.

The shared vision of our cultural commonality coalesces in the truth that we've fully entered the *Age of the Individual*—in which we are all living primarily for ourselves, far from a community-based society, and not as a family-oriented society, as we'd like to believe, but as an individual-oriented society. Maybe that's The American Dream, because it sure seems to be what we're dreaming these days. With our ever-increasing societal population, we have migrated away from small towns and more indigenous or family-oriented lifestyles into humungous and impersonal city-groups, in which the focus is moreover on our individual concerns.

Ironically, another aspect of our common unity is the pain, isolation, and exhilaration that living in the *Age of the Individual* entails.

However, the pain also has a unifying and potentially healing effect as we share the common plight of our "planet in peril," our concerns of global devastation that the modern industrial way of life has engendered. Paradoxically, we have detrimentally affected the planet so dramatically that we now each have a more global awareness of our impact on the earth. This change, brought on by technology, has given the impression that humankind is gradually becoming *a planetary and global community,* imbued with our concerns about the health of the planet—because our very lives depend on it!

Technology is beginning to realize that it must save life on earth from *itself.* The destructive aspects of industry and technology have progressed so dramatically in the past one hundred years that its creative aspects are now being called upon to provide solutions to the damages we've done to the planet, to increase the likelihood of future global ecological stability, and to expand the consciousness of human beings.

Due to recent developments in technology, many people around the world now feel a shared responsibility for the earth at large—not just their own boundaried country, culture, or continent—as our individual fates are becoming more closely intertwined with the fates of all human beings, cultures, and countries, as with the fate of the earth.

Through living the *Age of the Individual* to its extreme, we're beginning to pass into an age wherein the individual is becoming inextricably interconnected with the collective group or whole of humanity.

In this way, *we are progressing into a new era of global community.*

In achieving a greater sense of global unity, the day is dawning when we will all primarily consider ourselves to be "Earthlings," and our new identification with a *global community* will eradicate the need for war. We tend to become unified by a common threat, and the largest common threat these days is the deterioration of the planet. We are now beginning to unite against this threat, which is really the threat of the destructive aspects of our modern industrial and imperialistic progress.

With a little hope and understanding, we could work together like the United Nations to seek interrelated, interracial, intercultural, interreligious, hybrid ways of living that incorporate the entire panorama of modern technologies and ancient spiritualities into new ways of living into the future that inspire health, healing, and love.

I believe this potential shift in thinking, being, and behaving also involves a shift in focus from money and materialism to a focus on those qualities of life and being that inspire us to live and to cohabitate this planet. While money is the medium of the madness, we our slowly forcing ourselves to transcend our selfish short-sightedness and to break out of the shell of our material paradigm back to a way of being guided by the essential invisibles, the unseen spirit, and the underlying meaning of our purpose on the planet.

XIX

WALKING THE CAR
OR DRIVING YOUR BODY?

I LIKE TO WALK AROUND outside because life in a box gets dull. I walk wherever I can, on streets and sidewalks through neighborhoods right on down through town, and on the beach or in the woods where it is quieter and more beautiful. It's good to get outside, to smell the fresh air, to feel the sun or the night sky, listen to the birds or the crickets, to see and sense the surrounding world, and sometimes even say "hello" to other people. I like to walk because it is probably a human being's most natural activity. From time immemorial, walking has been our primary method of going anywhere—we forget that, on the grand scale of time, planes, trains, and automobiles are very recent modes of transport.

A spontaneous walk is not only good exercise; it's also a good form of adventure. In the house things are contained and stable, but once I step outside everything becomes more alive. Like an animal that has unfettered itself from a shell or a cave, once outside I am part of an entire planet and cosmos, keeping company with the sun and the clouds, the stars and the moon—the presence of celestial forces surround me, in the air and beneath my feet.

I've always loved walking and have wondered why there aren't more people like me walking around—for no good reason other than just to walk. By day it seems that people are locked up in their offices at work and by night they remain in the house, consumed by the television and domestic concerns. It's rare that I see another solitary individual, such as myself, just walking around outside—not in order to get somewhere, but just to walk. If I do, they are usually jogging.

I know that jogging is good for one's cardiovascular system and overall health, but, for me, jogging is too fast of a pace to be able to really appreciate my sensory encounter with the world. On a jog you can't stop to investigate curious details or *smell the roses.* For instance, while walking today I heard an enchanting sound and turned to see a woodpecker on the side of a telephone pole hammering away ... an incredible spectacle! And joggers never seem to be really enjoying their experience anyway because it's too much like work—they usually have headphones on listening to music to distract them from the discomfort of their efforts. Of course, there are joggers who appear to be happily immersed in jogging through the world; these joggers also tend to notice others and smile or utter some form of greeting as they pass.

Other than joggers, I also encounter people walking their dogs—I only hope that these people enjoy the walk as much as the dogs do. People out walking their dogs often times walk in pairs, are talking, and appear to be enjoying themselves. I think this is great and, when I am alone, some part of me envies them their company. Another part of me thinks maybe they are missing out on the solitary, meditative impact of a walk, during which an expansion of one's experiential awareness becomes possible— from a myriad fantastic perceptions of the surrounding world, to one's bodily sensations of breathing and walking, to the liberated flow of inner thoughts, inspirations, feelings, and imagination that is brought about by a steady movement of the body and mind.

In his book *The Miracle of Mindfulness*, the Buddhist monk Thich Nhat Hahn writes about awareness of one's breathing as the vital connection between the mind and the body. He suggests that when walking with a friend we resist the temptation of continual talk and instead remain mindful of our breathing, as well as our in-the-moment sensations which connect us with the world. I agree with Mr. Hahn that talking too much on a walk can greatly distract us from the wonders of the walk itself. When we're caught up in too much thinking, we leave the realm of the body and the moment of our contact with the living, physical world—which is our most direct experience of being alive.

Instead of walking outside, many people go to the gym for physical exercise. They walk or run on treadmills while watching a television or listening to their iPod, thus more completely distracting their minds and disconnecting their awareness from their bodies—while also disconnecting their bodies from the natural surrounding environment. They also engage in other forms of fitness training activities such as lifting weights, swimming, and aerobics. While all these kinds of exercise are wonderful for the health and conditioning of the body, I am quite certain that none of them are adequate substitutes for activities enacted outside, in a natural environment.

In the man-made, enclosed *box-environment* of a fitness center or gym, the body becomes more or less abstract; removed from its natural environment, it is thus placed in a *laboratory* in which it is viewed as a sort of *experimental object* that must be worked on in certain ways—like a car—to achieve certain results. While this is completely valid and effective according to our aesthetic and health goals, this attitude towards the body is rather mechanical, lacking the profound dimensions of interaction with nature wherein the body is immersed and engaged through all the senses with a living, spirited world that feeds the deeper portions of our souls.

Over the years, alongside our technological developments, we have radically diminished our contact with the earth and profoundly reduced the effect the natural world has upon our bodies, minds, and souls—but on those occasions that we go outside and *re-member* our primal connection with the earth through a direct embodied encounter, we are often, once again, awed. This is why it is so extremely important to get out of *the box* of our culture, out of the house, car, building, and limited mind-space in which we habitually dwell, and into nature from time to time.

The truth is, we came from nature, we are nature, and we experience ourselves more fully and fulfillingly when we are engaged with nature. As children we were instinctually aware of this, but as adults we need to consciously remember it.

WALKING ALONE PRESENTS an opportunity for the perfect intersection of self and world, like two circles that partially overlap one another creating a third elliptical-shaped space like an eye, by which the merging of the two worlds envisions a third. Walking alone provides an occasion for both adventure and meditation, an activity whereby continuous, ongoing, *in-the-moment* sensory perceptions and self-reflections are developed through direct contact of self with world.

In this day and age of the "auto-mobile," however,—in which we *automatically mobilize* ourselves, thereby entering a state of *auto-pilot* that anesthetizes the body—walking is usually a choice and not a necessity. In reality, travel by car is both a luxury and a torment. We drive the car daily, or take the bus, train, or airplane, covering such large distances that most of us no longer think about walking as a valid form of transportation. Because nearly everyone in the United States relies regularly on some form of engine or motor-based transportation, we take their very existence for granted. And because we grew up with cars, in a *car culture*—you have only to recall how many thousands of commercials and ads you have viewed featuring the sale of cars—we consider cars as just another normal everyday aspect of our lives.

In addition to relying on cars daily, most of us also live near a road, from which the sight and sound of cars is ever-present. In this way, cars function as part of a *taken-for-granted background* against which we live the bulk of our modern human lives.

From the time we are small children, we're told to watch out for moving cars when we cross the street or go outside to play. We grow up riding in cars almost daily as passengers—to the store, to school, and to visit our friends and families—for a full 16 to 18 years before we ever get a chance to operate one. We're lectured by parents and teachers that safety is of utmost importance, and we have to study and pass a test to acquire a license to drive legally. When we first learn how to drive a car there is great novel amusement, as well as focus on driving correctly. After a couple of years, however, driving becomes *second nature*, as we drive almost every day.

Because cars have become such an ingrained aspect of our society, we rarely consider the complexity and magnitude of our dependence on cars until ours breaks down or we get into an accident. We rarely stop to consider the rather absurd fact that whenever we go somewhere in our car—which is typically whenever we go anywhere when we leave the house—we enclose ourselves in a tremendously massive hunk of steel, glass, plastic and rubber, a contraption that employs an engine which burns up ancient fossil fuels that have been sucked out from very deep inside of the earth and that, when burned, are emitted into the air as toxic fumes.

The car is a kind of mobile vault, a room with a view onto the moving world, upon which we are utterly dependent because our world does not value the capacity of our own bodies as adequate vessels of locomotion. We rarely stop to consider how much drastically more is involved in driving a car as compared with walking. We rarely stop to think about the fact that when we drive our car on the freeway we travel at speeds much faster than any one of us can run—we'd rather not think about the dangers involved with traveling at such high speeds and velocities.

We rarely stop to consider that we are the only species on the planet that has devised a *second body* which we regularly inhabit and operate from within, while being transported at incredibly high speeds and negotiating complex adaptations to other cars and their drivers. Driving a car on the freeway at full speed feels very normal to us; however, if you've ever broken down on the side of the freeway you became quickly aware of the very tremendous and frightening force of all the other cars roaring past you. You also probably became aware of the fact that, should any of the cars suddenly swerve and hit you, your life would surely come to an end. It is during moments like these that the distinctly non-human quality of motor vehicles becomes overwhelmingly apparent. The cars noisily pummeling by you appear to be some form of alien creature with absolutely no capacity for feeling or empathy regarding your precarious situation.

I ONCE ATTENDED A WORKSHOP led by Malidoma Somé. Before arriving at the site in Boulder, CO he traveled by car from the airport in Denver, about an hour's drive away. He mentioned that during his ride in the car, as he looked out at the other cars on the freeway, he had to remind himself that each car had a human being inside who was driving the car. In his mind, a car was something really unrelated and foreign to a human being. He saw the crowded swarm of cars on the freeway for what they were: machines. In and of themselves lifeless, unfeeling, inanimate, and utterly strange.

Malidoma told us that from an indigenous cultural point of view, *the world of machines epitomized by cars is a very weird world in which one's humanity may be lost.* In his own words, "Indigenous people are indigenous because there are no machines between them and their gods." Although he has lived a good portion of his life in the tribal village of Burkina Faso, West Africa, Malidoma Somé is not a naïve newcomer to modern society—he has also spent many years in Europe and the United States, and attained Ph.D. degrees at Sorbonne and Brandeis University. However, throughout his teachings, Malidoma warns that modern technological society maintains the propensity to devour the soul and the spirit of our humanity by its extensive focus on the very machines and devices we have made essential to our way of life:

> Those serving the culture don't have the option to slow down and address the issue of what to do with their own needs, or how to get in touch with their own unexpressed powers. For they are too caught up in the speed and motion that is required by the Machine to feed its overt power. But some ultimately become so distraught that they figure out a way to take care of themselves rather than to take care of something that can never be satisfied.

Although this quote is directed at the whole of modern technological society, it can also be used to understand our relationship with cars as a sort of epitome of the modern person's experience of our machine-based way of life. Are we driving the car or is the car driving us? Are we in control of this world of technology or is the world of technology now controlling us? Who is really at the wheel? What has happened to the soul of our humanity which has been forced to live within the demanding confines of a mechanized, machine worshipping world? A world in which cars are both mandatory and menacing—destroying the environment while also destroying many human lives, instilling chronic anxiety, frustration, and rage into our daily state of being.

We say that cars are indispensible to our way of life and future progress, but what we really mean is that traveling large distances as quickly as possible is indispensible to us. And in some way, this overwhelming need to remain in perpetual motion belies our discomfort with being still. Malidoma claims that "speed is a way to prevent ourselves from having to deal with something we do not want to face."

In our obsession with speed, movement, and velocity, what is it that we are avoiding? Perhaps it is our weakness, our vulnerability, our helplessness in the face of a mechanized culture that largely has no interest in our personal concerns. Our bodies are composed of flesh, blood, and bone, not steel, glass, and rubber; they are animated by the mysterious forces of creation, not by fossil fuels. Yet, through cars and other man-made technologies, we have created a world of machines that is ultimately non-human and, in many ways, is physically, emotionally, and spiritually destructive.

When driving or riding in a car, it could be said that one's body is not really moving through space, as one is encapsulated in the spacial domain of the car. One sees the unfolding sensory world passing by, but is not in direct contact with that sensory world.

I do not think that life was originally designed to be experienced in a sitting position, encased in a steel machine, and viewed from behind a windowpane, "through a glass darkly." Yet how much of our lives is spent in this manner, whether in the car, the office, the airplane, or the living room?

When walking, one's body occupies the natural, open, *universal space* that connects all living beings. When traveling in a car, one is removed from that space, enclosed within another, infinitely smaller space from which one may *objectively* view the surrounding world. This is just another way in which modern technology distances human beings from the earth and the body from nature, enforcing upon us greater and greater separations from an original, firsthand, direct, and engaging contact with life, which—up until just about a hundred years ago—we had retained for thousands and thousands of years.

Although I prefer walking over driving whenever I can, I realize that we live in a world that necessitates machine transport in order to participate in many social activities. However, as a culture, I believe we would benefit by remembering that our own legs are often times the best way to travel. I hope one day we are able to reshape our lives, through reshaping our towns and our relationship with our bodies, in ways that respect our instinctual needs, the diversity of our bodily senses, and our innate connections with planetary life.

XX

AN INSIDIOUS EXPERIMENT UPON MAN'S MOST PRIMAL INSTINCT

IN MANY INDIGENOUS CULTURES in tropical regions clothing is not designed to cover up or hide parts of the body, except, at times, the genitals. Perhaps, because public nudity is not taboo in these cultures, the appearance of the naked body does not elicit such a strong response from the opposite sex or invoke a judgmental eye from the overriding societal moral conscience in general. But in our modern culture the naked body is a private matter and not allowed to be *exposed* in most public places. As a result of our societal taboo against and criminalization of public nudity, we of the modern world have been collectively denied the most natural expression of who we are: the free and sensuous fulfillment of our physical nakedness. By this, I mean an open, non-secretive, and non-shameful experience of our body's natural state of being, an experience that does not imply sexual activity, but rather encourages an appreciation of our physical, sensational contact with the natural world—and even, God forbid, with one another.

Indeed, the modern human species is the only creature upon the planet that demonstrates such a striking uncomfortableness with its own flesh and bone, with its own physicality, its own body. Strangely, we've come to accept this state of affairs and rarely pause to question why it has come to be.

Perhaps the biggest cause for our rejection of the physical self is that we've been conditioned to believe that physical nakedness is equivalent with sexuality, and that public physical nakedness is equivalent with moral indecency. Why else would we feel so ashamed and embarrassed to be seen naked and without clothing by others? Cats and dogs do not wear clothes; neither do birds or fish or bears or termites. Yet we of an infinitely greater and more creative capacity for intelligent thought have somehow arrived at the profound conclusion that our bodies must not be revealed to others en masse, that the physical flesh of the body is either too sacred, too secret, or too shameful to be an ordinary aspect of our daily social lives. Thereby, we've been entrained by rules and regulated by shame to only disrobe indoors where no one else might glimpse our naked bodies, except our lover.

An exception to this rule is the nakedness condoned in the doctor's office for a medical examination—where it is okay to reveal our physical nakedness to another person in a public place for purposes of consultation if we think there might be something *wrong* with our body or we are sick; yet it is not okay to be naked in public for purposes of simply enjoying the good health of our bodies unburdened by clothing. This partial exception to the illegality of public nakedness also reveals our underlying attitude of *maintenance*, rather than celebration, of the body. Thus, we have repressed many of the natural joys and sensational pleasures of the body, and numbed ourselves to the point that we only really pay attention to our bodies if we are in pain or sick.

Of course, there are also nudist colonies and nudist beaches. But even the term "nudist" implies some kind of semi-morbid deviant enchantment with something that is considered to be socially aberrant. And yet the very idea and assumption that the body must be clothed to be "decent" denotes a perplexing mode of thinking that casts a looming shadow of *badness, wrongness,* and *suspicion* upon the body itself.

In physical terms, *we are a body.* Therefore, the underlying message of this way of thinking about the body is: "Who you are cannot be seen! Who you are must be hidden!" The shame in this line of thinking about the body is alarmingly obvious.

This idea that nakedness is wrong insinuates that there is something inherently wrong with us as physical creatures. Perhaps in all our glorification of the rational mind we have enacted a subconscious violence against the body which also mirrors our destruction of nature and our generally oppressive attitude towards the other animals.

As a result, we have learned to both repress and sexualize our bodies. Yet, the body is neither bad nor altogether sexual. A better word to describe the body and its faculties is perhaps sensual or sensuous. Indeed, the body is a highly sensitive instrument as it *senses* the surrounding and internal environments. The sensuousness of the body includes its ability to breathe in the fragrant aroma of a flower or listen to a symphony of birds or to enjoy the tactile feel of a leather jacket. The sensuous world which the body inhabits is inclusive of sexual experience, but is by no means limited or defined by it. Yet our social rejection of our nakedness appears to make this confusing association explicit.

If modern Western society did not repress the body, thus making its naked and natural state some kind of hidden mystique and enigma, and if the truth and the reality of the body were accepted, allowed, and acknowledged instead of criminalized in our culture, there would be less tension and concern around when and where we are naked or clothed. (In this case, clothing would serve an optional, utilitarian, and or expressive/artistic need, but not a legal mandate.) However, the taboo against the naked body is both symptomatic and symbolic of a larger, more affecting and pernicious taboo, a taboo against *being who we are*, a taboo against many of our most natural and inherent impulses, instincts, emotions, needs, desires, and everything that is authentic about us though not acceptable in the eyes of society.

The struggle to come to terms with ourselves within the limitations placed upon us by society is constant, resulting in a neurosis of the individual which reinforces a conflicted society. There seems to be no real, apparent reason why the natural, naked human body should be outlawed, other than that we have projected our shame, embarrassment, and restricted terms of ownership and privacy upon it. I guess we can just chalk it up to being another one of modern civilization's great achievements: the very skin in which we live is now considered to be contrary to the concerns of our culture, making us all criminals at birth who must hide ourselves beneath layers of clothing.

On another level, this kind of thinking symbolizes our worship of capitalism and manmade things over nature and our inherent, earthly rights and pleasures. In order to be a member of the modern human society, you have to deny the body its freedom of expression.

This sort of agreement we make to virtually unspoken laws causes us to recoil from the more basic, physical, earth-centered modes of reality, and instead to keep ourselves locked up in the house watching TV or glued to the computer, surfing the internet, emailing or chatting on Facebook, a million miles away from the dirt and the dust and the wind and the rain and the lonely earth that howls and languishes just under our noses.

Because nakedness in the modern world is not an option—unless one goes to the strip club, which is a supreme example of the sexualization of the body—we are compelled to purchase all sorts of physical adornments. Further, we are judged by our attire, placed within a social status and rank based on the cut of the clothes we wear (not to mention the car we drive). In this way, our rejection of our physical nakedness becomes a force of dehumanization. Yet when you strip the man of his clothing, underneath we are all the same vulnerable, beautiful, majestic human being.

What is it that differentiates our society, in which there is a prohibition of nudity, from pre-Western or indigenous cultures, in which nudity is a normal aspect of life and does not elicit *sexual madness or depravity*? Perhaps in cultures that do not have a neurotic relationship to the body, physical nakedness does not equate with sexuality or sex, and sex or sexuality does not equate with moral depravity. However, modern culture, as evidenced by our sexualization of the body and our criminalization of public nudity, appears to connect these three distinct modes of being. By doing so we have concocted a recipe for complete and utter psychological disaster. We have devised an insidious experiment upon a human being's most primal instinct.

IT IS BOTH IRONIC AND INSANE that modern society condones the depiction of violence—in an exquisitely colorful palate of variety, throughout a broad spectrum of media, art, and entertainment—though most any depiction of nudity is automatically censored or considered to be *adult material*. This trait demonstrates our preference and appetite for destruction and desecration of the body over an appreciation for or ability to acknowledge and enjoy the body.

It seems that many of the joys and pleasures we are capable of experiencing through the body have been labeled by the puritanical paradigm as *sinful*—the sensuous and desiring body equated with the devil, and the idealistic, contemplative mind angled towards *the spiritual realm* of God. It is as if we are compelled to express our dislike, animosity, and even hatred for the body, and repress our acceptance and love. But when a society prefers violence over love—especially for something as essential as the body—you can bet there is something profoundly wrong with the heart and soul of its people.

Perhaps the distorted Western way of thinking about nakedness and the body begins with the biblical story of Adam and Eve, in which, after eating the fruit of the Tree of Knowledge of Good and Evil, both Adam and Eve became suddenly aware and ashamed of their nakedness. Before this, they had supposedly lived more or less in tandem with the other creatures of the Garden, but from that point forward they became separated out through a painful process of drastically expanded self-consciousness.

Many would agree that to be conscious of oneself or to be self-aware is a good thing. So why did the shift and expansion of consciousness for Adam and Eve lead to a state of existential anxiety and shame in which they felt impelled to cover up their original nakedness? To a condition of *Paradise Lost?* It seems that we of European descent have lived in this fearful and protective state regarding our nakedness—our naked bodies and our naked souls—ever since ...

Looked at allegorically, the story of Adam and Eve's fall from the Garden of Eden portrays humankind's shift from a state of childlike innocence, wonder, and unity into the difficult and sometimes brutalizing process of individuation through which human beings become specifically aware and conscious of who and what they are, and wherein their *naked and vulnerable* condition becomes magnified a thousandfold. As the old saying goes, "Ignorance is bliss."

According to the Bible, humankind's expulsion from the Garden of Eden was a result of the *original sin*—Eve's eating of the forbidden fruit—through which we lost our *original connection* with God, and thus began the quest to redeem ourselves and regain our *original unity* with all of creation. Seen from this viewpoint, our ensuing challenge has been to incorporate an expanded awareness into our consciousness. Could it be that in some very rudimentary ways modern humankind has failed to accomplish this necessary task, thereby criminalizing nakedness and promoting the development of *fashion games* that are played out upon our ambivalence towards nakedness and sexuality?

The same argument could be made for the criminalization of certain natural, hitherto magico-religious sacramental plant substances like marijuana, peyote, and psilocybin mushrooms, now called *drugs*—such labeling is a devious attempt to redefine them with negative intonations—because exploration of these substances transports the mind, the body, and its senses into altered states of consciousness, or altered states of *being*, wherein new knowledge and new dimensions of experience become available to the experimenting individual.

The message given by our authoritarian, police-ruled society regarding both nakedness and *drugs* is clear:

This knowledge is not okay.

This knowledge is not allowed.

In many cases, *such knowledge* is penalized by days, months, or years in the insane asylum of incarceration, followed by the lifelong negative branding accomplished through assuming a criminal record. This message, and the corresponding penalty—that of an exclusion and excommunication from the normal realm of society for a period of time, followed by a lifelong marking of estrangement—bears striking resemblance to the one given by God to Adam & Eve for their act of original sin in the Garden of Eden.

Criminalizing public nakedness appears as another attempt of Western society to distance the human being from the earth.

(Most outdoor areas in which we might encounter nature, such as parks, hiking areas, and beaches are all public places.) This makes us more estranged from ourselves and impels us to cling to the mind, to mental constructs and beliefs, instead of abiding in a direct knowing of ourselves through our bodies as earthly creatures upon this miraculous planet. Indeed, such direct experience or interface between our bodies, our consciousness, and the earth is inextricably interwoven with the depths of our souls.

In pre-Western, indigenous cultures, the concept of the individual exists more or less as inseparable from the group, as intrinsically interwoven with and belonging to the group and to the ecology and the spirit of the earth.

Thereby, it is reasonable to suppose that within such cultures the body in its natural, naked state also, in a general and unspoken way, belonged to the group as well. In other words, the body as a holy vessel of life is understood to be The Body or The Divine Body. To shame, hide, or deny the body would be tantamount to inflicting the same rejection and repression upon the Creator. Such a thing would be considered to be insane.

Contrastingly, in modern Western society the individual is clearly demarcated and differentiated from the group, set apart and distinguished as an *emancipated* entity with a complete set of rights, as well as obligations.

Correspondingly, one's body is considered to be one's own *private property*, one's most primary and singular possession. Although, ironically, it cannot be freely shared or expressed with the group at large ...

XXI

ILLEGAL ALIENS TO
UNIVERSAL EARTHLINGS

IN MODERN SOCIETY the concept of the body as private property expands to cover the clothing we wear; the car we drive; the room, apartment, or home we rent or own; the food we eat; and, of course, the money we earn. But perhaps, historically, the most important concept of private property extends to the land we occupy. This is historically significant to those of European descent—English, Spanish, Portuguese, French, Danish, etc.—who came to the American continent and raided the land, dispensing with its native inhabitants as they pleased. Those Europeans conquered and claimed this land as their own *private property*, and now their descendants ration and sell it for great sums of profit.

These days, most nations around the world, including the United States and the United Nations, recognize such invasive actions as criminal and do not tolerate them. However, the foundation of our country is historically based on such atrocious behaviors that resulted in the horrific decimation of hundreds of thousands of Native Americans and their cultures—from Canada down through the United States and Mexico into South America. To mention these facts makes most modern Americans uncomfortable and defensive, like the apparition of the rejected alcoholic or drug-addicted family member who occasionally shows up at the front door, homeless, dirty, and desperate; nevertheless, they are facts we should not forget.

In the United States, now that we have asserted and solidified our continued *state* of dominion over this land and all who reside within it, we have become very sensitive and concerned as to who is allowed entry. On the one hand, we are worried about terrorist invasions and, stemming from mainstream explanations of the events that occurred on 9-11, further abominations of our culture and citizens.

If one accepts these explanations of the 9-11 catastrophe, this seems like a rational concern. On the other hand, in recent years Americans have expressed a great outrage over those we label as *illegal aliens,* mainly Mexican and South & Central American citizens who cross over *our* border to live in *our* country where it is explicated that they steal *our* jobs, tap *our* health care system, take advantage of *our* superior education, but don't pay *our* taxes, and generally use up resources that we'd rather horde for ourselves.

What we don't acknowledge publically in broadcast bravado is that these people are also incarcerated in *our* jails and prisons at astronomical rates and with no access to adequate defense attorneys. Nor do we like to mention the fact that the land now known as California, Arizona, and New Mexico was *their* land before it was *ours* and that, in truth, *we* are the *illegal aliens* who, like big bullies in the absence of parents, have not yet been called to consequence for our audacious transgressions against them.

Mexican culture has a familiar saying to those living in the border regions: "Mi casa es su casa." In English, this little saying simply translates as: "My home is your home." Mexican culture tends towards being very welcoming and generous in terms of hospitality. There is less of the "I, me, me, mine" that one often finds in the United States and moreover an ambience of inclusion, of family, and group-oriented consciousness.

I point this out to stress the difference in attitude and opinion of private property between Mexicans and Americans. Whereas our idea of private property is based on the stalwart image, or dare I say *mirage*, of the American pioneer turned enterprising capitalist; the Mexican idea of property is based less on private concerns and moreover hinged on a communal or community oriented consciousness in which the needs of one's group and family are tantamount to those of oneself.

The truth is, most of the Mexicans who cross over to the United States illegally do so out of need to support their materially indigent families in Mexico who have been ill-affected by European conquest of their land and culture. They work very long, strenuous hours on back-breaking labor jobs like picking fruits and vegetables all day in fields and landscaping or housecleaning work, performing tasks that most American citizens don't like to do, often at below minimum wage rates.

And yet, concerned, *patriotic* Americans feel somehow cheated by *illegal* Mexican workers. We exhort them to "Go back to your own damn country!" without really considering why they are impelled to come to the United States in the first place—other than to steal all the good things which we have worked so hard to procure.

Or should I say steal back the things we once robbed from them?

We don't like to recall the fact that Mexicans occupied this land long before Europeans came and took it over by force, using guns and slavery to instate our *superiority*. We don't like to consider that the European conquest of Mexican and South American land, culture, and resources has impacted these people tremendously, resulting in years of strife, societal breakdown, and turmoil, as well as the state of poverty in which they now reside. A poverty that is, in fact, based on the political regimes we have instituted as a replacement for their own. Our overall response does not appear to be as compassionate or inclusive as one would expect their response might be to us if the tide was turned.

Perhaps our self-protective and segregating attitude towards those persons who originate from *South of the Border*, whom we like to marginalize as *illegal aliens*, is just another destructive illustration of how in the United States we promote an exceptionally selfish culture, of how we think primarily in terms of ownership, private property, and self-aggrandizement.

Ah, that's right, it's all a part of our most marvelous invention: Capitalism!

In the United States, it's all about *my* life, *my* money, *my* education, *my* job, *my* house, *my* possessions, *my* assets, *my* retirement, *my* problems, *my* vacation, *my* wife and kids, *my* health, *my* illness, *my* life, and *my* death ...

You get the idea.

There's a lot of awareness and focus on "me"—and what I possess individually as a separate, distinct, and alienated individual—and not much on "we." So we—as a culture of *me's*—have become solitary, mysterious islands, separate bodies like planets or stars, occasionally colliding or grazing each other. The modern societal universe in which we live strangely replicates the scientific view of the universe itself—a vast, spacious, and empty place.

Although it's really a matter of perspective, as Alan Watts so elegantly articulated in his talks and writings, we've learned to identify with the *foreground* of life, with ourselves as individuals, and to ignore the *background*, which is everything that resides outside the focus of our awareness, the surrounding sea of humanity, nature, and life at large. Our entire social paradigm, our education, our economy, our politics, even our religion are all based on the perspective in which we emphasize our separations from others, how we contrast, stand out, and are unique.

This perspective, so well demonstrated in our philosophies of private property and capitalism, has also left *us* out in the cold, separate and disconnected from a greater reality, identity, and community with all living beings.

We tend to think that our practice of highlighting the individual as separate and distinct from the group challenges each of us to bring forth our greater potential—such as sales teams in which individuals struggle for the top sales position and receive incentives for the volume of their sales. However, we should also consider to what degree this separation from the group perverts or distorts the potential of the individual—by increasing our anxiety, stress, desperation, and feelings of enmity towards one another.

When the stock market crashes or the economy bottoms out, people become extremely distressed, even suicidal over the foreboding threat, or the paralyzing reality, of losing the material station in life that they have built up—just yesterday the news reported that a man who lost his job shot his wife and five children to death before killing himself. This sort of thing would not happen in a world that primarily emphasized our togetherness and mutuality as a society of people.

In the monumental, never-ending build-up of the individual, our sense of self becomes lodged in our "ego," in our image, our material accomplishments, and everything that makes us valuable to society. When something threatens our ego—our cherished self-images and corresponding feelings of self-worth—we become very insecure and desperate. With our cultural emphasis on the individual, we reinforce the ego, *the separate self,* the concept of who we are as rich or poor, wealthy or destitute, successful or failed.

Because we lack group cohesion as foundational to our identity, when we encounter desperate times and experience a devastation of our normal social status or sense of self we may feel there is nowhere to turn. Sadly, at such times, some of us turn against others or ourselves. Many of us don't feel comfortable turning to the group, to the community, friends, or even family when we feel so tragically down and out. We interpret our state of devastation as a sign of our failure.

At a deep, core emotional level we generally feel so unrelated to others, so caught up in our own self-heroic schemes, that when we're convinced we've failed we prefer to suffer alone rather than admit our wretched state to the world. At such times, instead of reaching out for support, we try to drown our misery by getting drunk, doing drugs, enacting violence, or jumping out the window of the 15th floor.

IF WE FELT OURSELVES TO BE more humanly connected with other people—if we experienced a deep sense of shared community—rather than set apart from one another as capitalist, consumer-based individuals, these sorts of economic and lifestyle devastations wouldn't take such a toll on us. Sure, they'd be profoundly upsetting, but not utterly and entirely overwhelming. However, because our society is founded on the principle of private property, by which we are held to very high levels of responsibility for ourselves, when we fall we fall hard, and we usually fall alone.

Although we maintain strong assumptions of the necessity of private property, it is possible for all of us to thrive together in relative, interrelated harmony, instead of chronic antagonistic opposition. And the truth is, although we of Western culture emphasize the individual over the group, even as individuals we have more in common than not. We all share the same basic needs and many of the same desires and goals. We just have different ways of expressing them. Perhaps, as a humanity we are evolving through this stage of extreme and exclusive focus on the individual so that we will eventually arrive at a more highly differentiated state of true community.

Indeed, humanity must evolve into an integrated way of life that includes both group consciousness and individual focus, in which we could just as easily experience our unity with others as we could our independence as differentiated beings. One could imagine a way of life that emphasizes *the context* in which individuals exist, how we fit in and are described by the larger picture or processes of life, as well as *the content* which we subsume as individuals, couples, families, and sub-groups. This perspective would emphasize our relationships and interdependence with others, the qualities we have in common and share, as well as our inseparability from *the world of others*, including people, plants, animals, land, nature, and cosmos.

By emphasizing a shared participation in the world, this way of life would highlight our shared responsibility for the world. Hence, compassion, not competition, would be the standard principle of living, inclusive of economy, within the vision of a shared and collective humanity.

Our reigning ethic and motto would be: "*If my sister or brother is hungry and suffering, then I am hungry and suffering*" or "*When I love my neighbor, I love myself*," instead of the "*Every man for himself*" doctrine of living that we currently espouse.

Such an evolved mode of human society would have less impetus for conflict, crime, and incarceration than our current society. There would be less of an atmosphere of *man against man* and *man against nature*, and more of an atmosphere of mutual support towards the shared vision that unites the individual with the group and the cosmos.

In this mode of living, humanity discovers itself functioning as an integrated whole in which all the different pieces and parts of the picture come together, in which all people of all races, sexes, classes, religions, and cultures are considered essential to the overall flourishing of humanity. And all of humanity is consciously integrated into a participatory awareness with all of creation, thereby experiencing itself as one aspect of another more complex matrix, that of life as a whole on this planet earth, and so on as a planet which dwells in a solar system within a limitlessly infinite universe.

In this mode of living, none of Creation is left out; everything is considered as an essential portion of a greater whole, as microcosm is to macrocosm. Nothing and no one is more or less valued or considered to be any more important or less essential to the overall process of life.

Is this image of a vastly more organized and integrated future global human society naïve, overly-idealistic, exceedingly liberal-minded, and quixotic?

Absolutely!

The thrust of this conception is really the integration of the modern paradigm of individuation with the ancient paradigm of interdependence that exists in group-oriented and earth-based cultures. From a collective unconscious to an individual conscious to a collective conscious that integrates the individual unconscious, the idea is that humanity is progressing along some inherent, organic path of development towards exceedingly greater levels, modes, or dimensions of wholeness and inclusivity.

I believe this process is an essential part of evolution which we must consciously pursue to continue living upon this planet in any kind of peaceful and loving manner.

XXII

VIRTUAL HUMANITY

TODAY I WENT TO THE BANK to consult with the banker about my account that appeared to be lower than I had thought—which always seems to be the case. I began talking with one of the workers who was very friendly and helpful. I asked her if I could see the recent activity on my account over the past week. She said she was happy to help me, but also asked if I did online banking at home. I told her I had done this a few times in the past, but not currently, as I did not own a computer. Her response was an understanding one, and she proceeded to help me.

As she pulled up my account on her bank computer, I commented on the stained glass windows embedded in the walls of the bank, and she said that the bank used to be a church. After a moment, I made a wry comment about how people are more concerned about money than God these days. She laughed, and I said, "But now you can pray while you work, right?" She laughed again, and commented on how people only need God when they're in trouble.

We continued our small talk as she printed out the sheet regarding my account, which cleared up my confusion by confirming that an automatic withdrawal for my car insurance payment had been made in the last couple of days. Eventually, I left happy and satisfied with her customer service and the quality of a human interaction.

Upon reflection, I realized that—regardless of all the persona and protocol involved—this interaction was essentially about *the human quality and capacity for relating and carrying on conversation*. As someone who values human interaction, I'm worried that if I relied only on home-based online banking I wouldn't have had this interaction with the banker.

I know it may seem petty and ridiculous for me to point this out, but in the modern world we are more and more often being directed by the advances of technological society to *interface* with computers instead of *interacting* with human beings, to stay at home and order or accomplish all we need via online internet shopping, banking, research, and living.

But, alas, if all our needs could be met *online*, none of us would ever have to leave the house to encounter one another at all. I'm concerned that this emphasis on the computer and the internet is becoming another threat to our humanity, to those daily, insignificant activities and encounters that make us human.

I'm concerned that we are gradually becoming a disassociated and mechanized society composed of isolated individuals gazing through our computers into the vast and endless, emotionally empty worlds of cyber-space, relying upon this ever-advancing technology to meet all our relational aspirations.

Maybe I'm just a throw-back hippie weirdo, but I still prefer a life in collusion with actual, physical, human beings—as well as other kinds of beings, like trees, squirrels and streams—none of whom can be directly encountered or experienced on the internet in a virtual or cyber reality. I appreciate the opportunities that the computer and online technologies offer, I just don't want them to take over my terrestrial human nature and turn me into a machine.

Do you?

XXIII

HOW ARE YOU?

"In your pathology is your salvation."
~James Hillman

WHEN TWO PEOPLE MEET they usually like to exchange greetings, such as "Hey, how are you?" or "How's it going?" or "Yo, what's up dude?!?" Usually these forms of greeting are interpreted moreover as alternate ways of saying "Hello" than as actual questions or queries into the other person's current state of being. But depending on how well the two people know each other, and how comfortable they are talking honestly about themselves together, the initial greeting can open a potential doorway into sharing one's immediate feelings or experience.

How the two people *respond to one another's responses* may also be instructive on the direction the conversation will take. With most of my friends, I tend to give basically honest answers to their greeting inquiry, inclusive of some kind of short report on how I'm doing or feeling, which may entail both the highs and lows of my recent internal barometer.

In the past, I was more careful about who I shared my true feelings and thoughts with, but these days I'm less guarded. However, on some occasions—should I express anything resembling sadness, anger, pain, or a feeling of loss—I'm still met with mild forms of protest or shock from the other person; although, for some reason people seem to be more comfortable with anger than sadness.

The gist of the other person's offended response is that *I don't need to feel what I'm feeling or think what I'm thinking*—even my thoughts are now called into question and labeled as "negative," or "a bad attitude." According to the other person, I should *think* of my situation differently, *feel* different feelings—the feelings that the other person thinks I should *choose to feel* rather than the one's I am actually feeling—or simply change my mode of perception. When I get this sort of response, I feel as if the other person has taken on the role of the Emotion Police, laying down the law on what feelings I am allowed to feel or express and what feelings or thoughts I should avoid at all cost. For some folks, feelings other than "fine, good, okay, and *couldn't be better!*" are totally out of the question.

In retrospect, it always strikes me as very amusing when the other person tries to talk me out of my sadness or anger—or any experience that they have labeled as *negative-thus-bad*—although, in the moment, it makes me feel antagonistic towards them. I appreciate that the other person, at heart, may only be really wanting me to feel better; however, I have the nagging suspicion that *they want me to feel better for them* more than for me.

To me, being authentic in my communications with others is more important than feeling good or putting forth an acceptable, glowing persona. It's both absurdly tragic, and somehow ridiculously humorous, that we human beings attempt to regulate our emotional capacities, mainly by pushing away anything unfamiliar, upsetting, or in any way painful, and by clinging on to all the familiar, safe, and pleasant feelings. Why are we so uncomfortable with sadness, with authentic feelings or expressions of grief, anger, fear, and emotional pain? Somehow our own discomfort at encountering genuine sadness, in ourselves or in others in the world, is telling of some process occurring below the level of our conscious awareness.

Traditionally, men are conditioned by parents, teachers, media, and one another to never reveal their sadness, while women are conditioned by these same authoritative forces to avoid expressions of anger. Although these social conditionings are intended to produce particular role identities that make sense for society, I believe they no longer have beneficial outcomes for Western civilization.

As mentioned previously, people in general seem to have greater tolerance for anger than sadness. Perhaps because we see so much violence on TV and in the movies we have become somewhat desensitized to anger. Ironically, it is more difficult to reflect upon, communicate, and discuss feelings of anger than to simply express anger reactively as we see done so frequently in the media. Indeed, our reactive expressions of anger may at times be our psychological defense mechanisms kicking in to protect our deeper and more tender areas of sadness, hurt, feelings of inadequacy, and other kinds of emotional pain. But, at times, feelings of sadness and sorrow may be a healing necessity, a form of nourishment that secretly feeds our inner self or a part of us that is authentically grieving a loss, tragedy, or some significant feeling of unfulfillment. We tend to think, conventionally, that happiness is the only worthwhile emotion, but we are far more dynamic beings than happiness alone can account for.

While modern Americans generally want things to be predictable, stable, and consistent in our actual everyday lives, we love forms of entertainment—TV soap operas, sit-coms, dramas, mov-

ies, 24/7 news programs, reality TV shows, and roadside accidents—in which people are consistently engaged in drama or
conflict, and otherwise behaving in overly emotional, histrionic,
and violent ways.

Why is this?

Do we need our emotional crises and upheavals in safely detached and objectified formats that the media conveniently provides us? Something draws us into these vicarious dramas of humanity, yet guards us against being intimately and interpersonally
involved in anything that affects us profoundly. Simultaneous
desire and fear engender internal conflict, leading us into uncanny states of fascination: we don't want to look at, or feel, what's
going on, but we can't look away, or turn off our feelings of interest. We want to feel fully and utterly alive, but we are afraid of
life, so we retreat from reality and watch the television instead.

Perhaps encounters with love and death are the most potent
and affecting dramas we will ever experience. The fact that we are
alive and will at some point die, that everyone we know and love
will die—or will otherwise leave us—regardless of our religious
conviction, is a pending mystery and suspense, an ultimate drama
that we face alternately with horror, hope, and vulnerability. Because we were all born into such finite and transitory lives, we are
all also subject to the dramas of death, loss, sadness, fear and
grief.

Recently, it's become fashionable for people to adopt the slogan, at times displayed on their MySpace, Facebook, or dating
site profiles, that they are "drama free." This is an amusing, in-
credulous little term, the epitome or penultimate statement of
denial regarding one's capacity for feeling and authentic thought.
If someone tells you they're "drama free" run the other way, because if they catch up with you, you're going to have more drama
than you know what to do with!

In short, such persons are lying. And their rejection of their own inner life will only make their outer life all that more conflicted. Sure, some of us are more relaxed and emotionally stable than others. But, on the other hand, sometimes these same people can also be rather empty, boring, and bereft of liveliness.

We will never, in this life, disentangle ourselves from the infinite complexities of the human drama, just as we can never escape the vast sea of emotions that inhabits our souls. Accepting one another's feelings and perceptions is more natural and harmonious than fighting or rejecting them. So if somebody tells you that they're sad or angry or scared or jealous ... acknowledge them for telling you the truth of what they are feeling. Don't try to make them feel something they're not feeling or something they don't want to feel. Don't try to make them feel like they should be someone they are not, because this will only make them feel worse.

Conflict occurs when we cannot accept one another as we are, when we reject one another's point of view, or invalidate one another's feelings. If you have difficulty accepting another person's feelings, you probably cannot accept your own. Instead of rejecting the other person, try talking about your own reactions to their feelings, or the difficulties you have accepting their feelings. In the end, your friend will respect you more you if you respect them and yourself.

WHEN YOU ASK SOMEONE: "How are you?" your question is like a key that can open a portal to that person's inner reality. So only ask the question if you're able to handle the potential response. You can't tell other people how or what to feel, so you shouldn't really have any expectations about the answers they give you when you ask. You've got to be open-minded. This applies to oneself as well.

Far too often, instead of accepting ourselves, we try to change what we feel or think or look like into something or someone we think we should be. But feeling *fucked up* or feeling pain is part of life—the tragic part which lives side by side with the comic and the heroic parts. When we deny our pain, we also deny our depths. We try to live in the make-pretend realm where society says we should live, but *to deny our darkness and our depths is as tragic as denying our joy.*

In reality, life pulls us underground from time to time—just as the seasons pull organic matter into the ground at specific times of the year—into painful places of confusion and turmoil, or perhaps not so much pain, but moreover *a darkened state in which mystery and the unknown prevail,* in which the light of the known world fades away. Instead of avoiding these areas of our lives, we could accept them as opportunities for inner growth, discovery, and magic. It's important to remain somewhat open and conscious during times of crisis, depression—*deep resting*—or descent into an unknown realm inside ourselves in which we encounter mysterious or even bewildering states of being.

All the intermittent little-deaths we experience throughout life have a lesson for us, a meaning for us to discern. Falling apart, breaking down, and being torn to shreds are all part of the Cosmic Game. Getting through these times, suffering through days, nights, months, or even years of these times is instrumental in making us who we are. These trials by fire and descent journeys contribute to our personal evolution as human beings.

Who would we be without our scars and our war stories? The times or moments in life which challenge us most radically are also those times or moments that define and describe who we are as unique individuals with significant and interesting stories to tell.

Life is a drama. An ongoing suspense film in which we can never truly predict what will happen next, either to us or through us, around us, or inside us. Though we like to believe we are *in complete control,* we are not—that wouldn't be very exciting anyways.

In life, as in death, there are no guarantees.

Stability is the still point of calm in the center of the cyclone, and we're fortunate to find a moment of reprieve or shelter from the storm whenever we can. For the most part, however, our lives are like rivers always moving into unprecedented territories. It's okay to feel a little out of control, or scared, or even desperate as hell from time to time. Fighting our uncomfortable feelings and states of being, instead of surrendering into them, usually engenders more distress than we had to begin with.

To be born is also to die, to enter into countless manifestations of *unknown wilderness.* We like to have peace of mind, but a philosophy of "pills for ills" denies us the broad range and vastness of our living human potential for dynamic feeling, expression, and experience—which manifest as both suffering and joy. When we judge and suppress pain and anguish, we also eschew pleasure and joy. Because you can't have one without the other. And when we attempt to control another person or ourselves, we lose the free flow of life that is essential to feeling alive.

XXIV

I WAS SPARED

A WEEK AGO I WAS RELAXING in my third story apartment preparing to hang a picture on the wall, when the earthquake came. It began as an increasingly rumbling movement of the entire building: the floor, the walls, and everything inside my apartment. Granted, I was hungover on this particular Sunday, but not nearly enough to account for convulsions of this sort. Feeling my whole world tremble and warble—as if the building was attempting to balance itself upon marbles of varying sizes—I quickly put down the framed photograph and instinctively grabbed onto the wall myself. At that moment, I truly felt helpless, unsure of what to do, fearing that the entire building would crumble and collapse with me inside it.

The quake lasted awhile, almost a minute—which is a long time when it comes to surfing your living room floor. When it was done, I still did not know what to do.

Should I run outside in case a larger quake comes?

Am I safe in here?

What the hell is happening?

I hadn't heard any forecasts for earthquakes that day. Maybe I should've watched the weather more closely.

Just outside my door I could hear people coming out of their apartments and into the hallway. They were exclamatory and talkative, but did not appear to be leaving the building. As I am not a California native, this sort of thing was not normal to me. So I just stood there silently, in shock, not knowing what to expect next.

Within a minute or two, a neighbor friend came down the hallway and called out my name, asking if I was okay. I opened the door to see her with another neighbor, beers in hand, smiling and chuckling—as if it were all some fun-loving prank they had played upon my Eastern-born innocence.

Upon seeing my face aghast, they both reassured me that we would be okay. Earthquakes like this happen all the time, they reasoned. I need not worry. My friend's consolation helped somewhat. The rest of the day passed, and a couple of hours later I hung the picture.

News reports later that day stated there had been a large earthquake, measuring 7.1 to 7.3 on the Richter scale, just south of the Mexican border near Tecate. Its rumblings had been felt as far as Los Angeles, and it had incurred two deaths as well as some slight structural damage to a few buildings in Mexico. A death of any sort, especially accidental, is a sad situation. Yet, all in all, for such a huge earthquake, no major structural damage had been done.

The conclusion of this story brings me to events that have occurred over the past twenty-four hours on the other side of the planet—a similar story of an even smaller earthquake which has had much larger and devastating consequences. I first read the report last night on the internet before going to bed and it prompted me to drink another beer.

In an area of Western China—actually the disenfranchised nation known as Tibet—an earthquake had just struck resulting in at least three hundred human deaths due to the demolishing of homes and buildings made of mud and wood. Perhaps the report was more poignant for me because I had just finished reading a book by the late Chogyam Trungpa Rinpoche, a Tibetan refugee of the Chinese invasion who subsequently spread the teachings of Tibetan Buddhism throughout the world.

However, anytime I hear about events of mass destruction I become both saddened and angry. It also always makes me question the existence of God, this notion that there is some all-loving, all-knowing persona, force, or entity in the sky who is responsible for all that happens in this grand universe.

It makes me wonder whether this God may indeed have some devil in him after all ...

Recalling how terrified I felt when the earthquake hit my home in Southern California, I imagine the Tibetan people who probably felt the same terror when their earthquake came, but then actually experienced the literal fragmentation of their world, many of them buried in the rubble of buildings, squashed and suffocated to death, helplessly trapped beneath the weight of the homes they had trusted, the homes which had been their places of safety. I imagine people being maimed: bleeding, broken bodies stranded in the streets, in shock and horror, not knowing what to do.

What's worse is the fact that these people who I am imagining are real. As I write this story they are suffering and dying, and I am powerless to help them. It's important to remember that the Tibetans are people just like you and me; they have skin, blood and bones, hearts and minds, identities and lives, dreams and a purpose upon this planet, just like us.

But for the past twenty-four hours many of them have been trapped under rubble, dying in agony, in hysterical horror—or perhaps in dignified surrender—helpless to counteract their fate.

Thinking about this makes me feel completely out of control. Heartbroken and furious all at once. And yet, somehow, I remain mute. Or am I muted by the forum and the policy of our culture to just report the news, with no real space or place in which to digest it, to make sense of it, to respond to it, to curse or condemn it, or to have any kind of relationship with it? I, we, all of us are more or less expected to just take it all in, all the reports of blood and mayhem, of tragedy and inconceivable human suffering, without doing or saying much of anything.

This sometimes really sucks.

Of course, I am incomparably lucky just to be alive, just to have the privilege of writing these words. The earthquake which hit my home had no measurable consequence other than freaking me out for a few hours. I was spared the utter calamity of destruction, the utter desecration of physical mutilation, and the ultimate finality of death, while others halfway around the planet were not.

It leaves me with so many questions:

Why was I so fortunate while others were doomed?

How can there be a God who would allow innocent people to be killed so mercilessly?

Is this the same God to whom I pray?

If so, how can I trust such a God? He or she may have a similar fate in mind for me ...

Troubled by the fallout of the earthquake in Tibet, I'm now troubled by my questioning of God. If there is a God—yes, I am now officially questioning my "faith"—why does God do nothing to help humans when we most need him or her?

How can I continue to pray to a Creator who would arrange a life for his or her creations in which there is such monumental misery?

And how can I continue to be a happy person, focused on my own life, when I am aware of such massive human suffering continually occurring around the planet?

We, as a privileged modern culture, tend to remain emotionless when we have access to news of these terrible events. Why is it so hard, so strenuous for us to even mildly admit to feelings of grief and madness when we hear of such calamity? (Yes, *madness*, as in out-of-control or out-of-your-mind *because tragedy just doesn't make sense.*)

It seems that our capacity for transmitting information has far outgrown our capacity to *sit with that information*, to understand and respond to it, *to feel it* and make some sense of it. In this, we run the terrible risk of redefining knowledge as information, as something that we experience only with the very tops of our heads and the nerve endings most remote from our hearts and our guts.

As a culture, we want to surmise the entire globe. We want unlimited access to information of activities from the point of view of disinterested observers. Is it our chronic state of inner emptiness that motivates us towards this need to be constantly *informed* by the continuously riveting news of *external* events? We have glorified and literalized the scientific method beyond reason, applying it to daily life situations which carry no meaning for us unless we dive in completely and become immersed.

As the Sufis say, "Reality is in the tasting."

Perhaps we also are afraid, really, to *allow Reality to taste us.* And yet, perhaps that is why we must also have our own tragedies—both personal and collective—from time to time, because only through some portion of death can we truly feel the full impact of life.

The Tibetans and the Buddhists in general have a particular prayer-mantra that they circulate regularly through their minds and hearts.

It goes something like this: "May all beings be free of suffering. May all beings be at peace."

I like this particular prayer as it really has universal implications. It is not just a prayer for oneself or one's own concerns. It is a prayer for all sentient, living beings, for all life everywhere upon this planet and, potentially, throughout the universe. It is a prayer of compassion for the well-being of all things. As such, it implies a universal unity, a wholeness and acceptance of all life as essentially interrelated.

For those of us living in the Southern California and Mexico border region who felt our world tremble just a week ago, remember, we were spared.

We have lived while others have not.

Remember how fortunate we are just to be alive while others go homeless, their lives shattered or suddenly and violently ended altogether.

And while remembering this, send a little love to those less fortunate folks who have been praying for us our whole lives. Perhaps it's time we remember them and pray for the sanctity of our human race. For, in essence, we are them and they are us.

XXV

LAST NIGHT I DREAMED

Last night I dreamed that I befriended a big grizzly bear. I lived out in the dark rainy night with him in a field overgrown with small trees and scrub brush. We ended up in someone's home and I kept him from eating a naked man alive. The bear and I could not avoid civilization and our clash with it. We needed food.

HAVING STUDIED a little psychology, I realize this dream would be a field day for a Freudian. Sitting here upon the couch—not the Freudian couch, but my own little futon model—I can still see the burly, slick fur of the bear out there in the dark rainy night, in a field between plots of neighborhoods and homes. I feel his firm, rough presence standing beside me.

Now that I'm fully awake, I wonder: *What the hell was I doing in a field, at night, in the rain with a big grizzly bear?* From what deep and distant cave of my nocturnal dreaming mind did this burly bear tread? In the dreamscape of my psyche, which felt and appeared as real as any reality I've known, we were like refugees unable to escape the surrounding stranglehold of modernity. And yet, I felt tremendously alive in that green field of bushes, trees, and overgrown scrub, outside in the dark, rainy night with that bear.

The Freudian would tell me that the bear is symbolic of some portion of my own unconscious soul, that a part of me identifies with the bear—a wild creature whose sighting terrifies the civilized world of humans. The Freudian might even laugh a little at the fact that I have to keep the bear from eating a naked man alive—noting the humor to be had from the polarity between these two dream figures. He or she might note the dream's symbolic commentary on how vulnerable modern man is to his animal instincts, how easily we can be devoured by our own *grizzly* impulses.

Yet the Freudian would also be careful not to demean the figure of the bear, but to envision the dream from the bear's point of view as well, to see the bear's attempted attack upon the naked man as an expression of his innate drive for homeostasis, stemming from the fact of his exclusion from human society—and the threatening encroachment of that society upon his own habitat. He might even go a step further and interpret that whoever has dreamed this bear is experiencing some significant inner conflict between his id and his ego, between the unconscious and conscious portions of his mind, or between his instincts and his conscience.

Of course, not being a Freudian myself, I am imagining all these Freudian responses. In reality, I cannot afford to consult a psychotherapist about my bear dream. So, I must be my own Freudian analyst and bare myself to the blank page, as to an unseen audience of readers who I can't imagine very well. Perhaps, as Jung would say, I am also becoming my own analyst by *dreaming the dream onward.*

Either way, the dream demonstrates that I am befriending the figure of a wild grizzly bear. At some point, perhaps I will bring him to a party and introduce him to all my friends. Hopefully he won't try to eat them.

The dream also tells something about the difficult redemption found through keeping company with wild things in a world of mundane, urban environments. Indeed, there is something profoundly "anti-animal" about the blueprint and execution of modern day neighborhoods.

Where is the wildness in the design—let alone the function— of most modern day homes, yards, offices, schools, churches, shopping centers, restaurants, and hospitals? Perhaps this is why the sudden discovery of a bear is all the more sweet and invigorating to the soul.

In the profusion of our sterile modern day aesthetics, we've demonstrated to the bear—both the one in the world, and the one in our psyches—that there is little room, if any, for him or his energies to thrive in our world. We've delineated the figure of the bear to the graveyards of our psyches, to the outer zones, the fringes of society where the drunken dropouts, the homeless, and the mentally deranged also reside.

(Consider that in our modern society the graveyard is one of the only places left that retains some fundamental element, some trace of grizzly wildness through its association with death, with grief and endings, with the unexplainable communions between the here and now and the ever after, between this world and the next, between the unseen inner realm of hearts and souls that feel so deeply it is as if their weight would take us down to the very bottom of our oceanic psyches, beneath all that is seen, to a place where reality is primordially self-evident and not manufactured or fabricated by fucked up, insecure human egos.)

If there is no room, no place for wild things, for wildness, wilderness, and figures of the dark in our blueprint, our conceptual philosophy of human society and our daily experience of modern culture, then how can we begin to acknowledge the figure of the bear or our own animal nature that lives inside our dreams and our souls?

In external modern human society, the wild animal has become criminal, outlawed, is hunted down and shot, or sedated and relocated to safe preserves miles away from our normal routine. How can we possibly function in such colossal denial of our interrelationship with the other creatures of this planet? Doesn't such a state of denial obfuscate who and what we truly are as living beings dependent upon the earth?

When we cannot honor and acknowledge the wild forces around us, how can we honor and acknowledge the wild forces that live inside us?

Indeed, how bereft we have become of our planetary brothers and sisters! How isolated from the wild world of animals and elements, rocks and weeds, dirt and bees, buffalo and bears, from EVERYTHING that surrounds our flimsy, ungracious construction of human habitation. We have forced the bear to break into the house of our unconscious and appear as an intruder to be acknowledged.

In our own exclusively human culture, we've demeaned the bear's existence to a television portrayal of cartoons, or even worse, as living in a zoo. Yet, in our internal world, he lives freely, beyond the heavy hand of our repressive urges and is wandering wildly through the dreamscape of our slumbering psyches.

The naked man in my dream is completely vulnerable and at odds with the bear because he is hiding inside his home in a state of chronic self-protection, afraid to go beyond the scope of his own tidy lawn. As a modern human society we have demarcated our territory so sharply and abruptly that there is little overlap between the wild world and the human realm, between the unconscious soul and the conscious mind. These days, there is more or less a cut-off, a division, a "No Trespassing" sign between the two. And our *civilized society mind* keeps encroaching further and further upon the wild realm of our inner instincts, our feelings and our freedoms, our natural energies, tendencies, and impulses.

Modern man is eclipsing himself with his own fear of life, alongside his obsession with the fantasy of total control based on a sense of logic and order that is truly irrational. But the unruly, wet, primordial, instinctual, non-verbal animal nature of our unconscious inner reality remains to remind us of who we really are down deep beneath all the meaningless and incessant idiocy.

AT NIGHT THERE IS a small red light outside my window. It seems to be perched up high upon something in the midst of an ocean of shadows. The red light is a single flaming eye, a small pinprick through to the heart of universal wild energy. The red light cannot be explained, rationalized, or reduced down to reason and logic. It simply is. And it cannot be truly destroyed, only at times covered over by shadows. Perhaps some of us stop seeing the red light, but like the inexplicable hot beating of Life upon this planet, the small red light will never be extinguished, until the day the sun engulfs us completely ...

Epilogue

It's been over 5 years since I originally wrote the majority of this book, yet the perceptions, ideas, and insights around which it revolves remain the same. While digital technology is almost universally lifted up on a pedestal for mass worship, its underlying impact upon humanity, at least in the modern world, imposes an influence of distraction upon people that estranges us from one another, from our actual environment, and from ourselves.

Today it seems more people walking down the street have their attention glued to a handheld cell phone. And more people in public ignore one another as their fascination with their own handheld reality perseveres over actual face to face contact with other living people. Riding the bus, standing in line at the post office, even at the bar I find most folks gazing into their phones, some with ear buds blasting music so that they can all but entirely ignore their immediate surroundings. It is even quite common to see couples or friends at restaurants not talking, but texting other people, while their table conversation atrophies along with the quality of their relationships.

This, to me, is not the advancement or enlightenment of humanity. It is the decline of humanity, the decimation of humane living and the eradication of real human communication. When people in public habitually ignore one another, I think we as a society have gone astray. Many of you will disagree with me.

Evidently, on the whole, American society has chosen digital forms of reality over the *here and now* ordinary, physical, relational forms of reality in which we have always lived. However, this choice belies a profound conflict and gap within ourselves. No matter how ardently we engage with digital, virtual forms of reality, we cannot escape the fact that we are embodied creatures who breath air, eat food, drink water, piss, shit, exercise, have sex, talk and relate with other physical beings, and are the adventurous inhabitants of a complex and beautiful physical planet. In essence, we are deeply rooted in the physical world and can never escape it, hard as we may try.

The problem is not in the phenomena of digital realities themselves, it is in how we use them so exclusively and to the detriment of our other human capacities for being and relating. Time and again, we choose interactions with machines—computers, cell phones, iPods, iPads, Facebook, Netflix, video games, TV, etc.—over interactions with other human beings or animals or plants or our earthly planet. Why? Because machines are at our fingertips and we have a sense of control over them that is exhilarating. Yet, how can this preoccupation make us more human? And if having obsessive relationships with machines and digital realities does not make us more human, then what do they make us?

It seems to me that our very consciousness is slowly merging with machines, so that day by day we actually become less human and more mechanized ourselves, more digitally entranced, more robotic, more programmed and programmable ...

This portends a dangerous state of affairs and a foreboding outlook for humanity, culture, and society. Indeed, we have been and are every day becoming more programmed by the realm of technology via the media, the government, and the power structures ingrained in our society. As consumers, as law-abiding citizens, and as members of society who want to fit in with the cultural norms, we are intensely impressionable. Having become so engaged by digital forms of reality, we appear as automatons who all do the same thing. Nearly each and every one of us has been sucked into the technological grid, made dependent upon it for our very sense of identity, if not purpose in life.

It is difficult, painful, and at times infuriating to be in a room full of people who all have their heads, hands, and consciousness *ankle-deep* in their cell phones—ignoring one another! This state of affairs is simply wrong. It is anti-human, anti-humanitarian, and anti-life. It is profoundly alienating to be on the bus or at the bar or the coffee shop—it doesn't matter where, everywhere you go people are all doing the same thing—with a group of individuals who all simply ignore each other's existence and remain entranced like children to the TV within the sparkly glow of their handheld device. It's as if we have no mind of our own and no capacity to withdraw our attention from the technological realm—as if our human consciousness has been enslaved to a greater unseen "virtual" authority. It is maddening and deeply saddening.

An addiction is something we use to feel okay when we are not okay. It seems to me that our utter engrossment with digital media has become a profoundly serious addiction because we are not okay if we are not constantly *shooting up* with texting, email, online media, Twitter, YouTube, Facebook, etc. It truly is a sickness, a virtual mental illness!

Just last week I walked to a local bakery to buy a loaf of fresh baked bread. The bakery was also a restaurant in which there were many small tables and one large, group-sized table. As I waited in line to buy the bread I observed four individuals at the group table, each sitting at a corner—as physically far away from one another as possible. Each person interacted with a handheld digital device while ignoring the others at the table. One or two had ear buds on to block out listening to others as well. I felt perplexed, then outraged by this. I wanted to yell at them: "Stop ignoring each other! Get your face out of your phone and talk to your neighbor!" Of course, I didn't. But it was a clear sign of how the increase in technological society leads to a decrease in humanitarian society.

I left the bakery with visions of cafés in Greece and Italy, Costa Rica and Peru, where people are warm and inviting as they sit in groups or circles and smoke cigars and eat and talk for hours. I left wondering, *what the hell is becoming of our modern society!? How did we become such a cold, distant, detached, unwelcoming and alienated people??* It is disgusting how readily we isolate ourselves from others and refuse to participate in an open community atmosphere, even at the local bakery and café.

The irony is that our obsession with our cell phones as sources of information and digital communication is a kind of reaching out for connection, and yet the obsession makes us blind to the world that is right there in front of us and the other people we could be making connections with. These days, people are more apt to engage in the Facebook popularity contest of gaining "Friends" than they are in really talking with someone or spending quality time together—not merely texting or *digitizing* reality.

Sure, it's okay to have a digital reality, but it's really disastrous to allow your digital reality to obscure, depreciate, or eclipse your participation in direct, physical reality. Because you live in a body and you can't ignore it ... And you live in an actual society that you probably should not ignore either.

The problem with our relationship to new digital technologies is that we project our sense of community into them, along with the expectation that they will meet all our psychological needs. We engage a machine to expand our reality and experience of the world. But the world that awaits us inside a digital reality is not the same world that we live in, the world which surrounds us all the while. Yet we act as if it is—and to do so is a form of insanity. We eagerly check our cell phone for new texts, our computer for new emails, our Facebook account for new messages—as if the actual world that we live in is devoid of nurturing or friendship or intimacy. But looking to digital realities to resolve our psychological deprivations only worsens the problem. Our obsession with engaging digital reality represents our avoidance and denial of our unhappiness and unfulfillment.

So we walk through the world not as if we live in a community, but as if we have arrived in a strange place filled with undesirable people who we also avoid—because everyone who we don't know becomes a symbol of our own repressed alienation. But we always bring our security blanket with us, our transitional object—the cell phone—so that we have access to a familiar world in which known persons may contact us, or we them, in the safest and most least satisfying mode of communication we as a human species have yet invented. All the while the community around us corrodes and we do not become grander beings, we become smaller, less magnificent beings, less spontaneous and open to life, less connected with the universe of possibilities.

Digital reality, online media communication, email and texting are all modern miracles that enable us as a society to achieve levels of communication that are amazing. Nonetheless, we shouldn't let technology obscure or even blur the ancient miracle of being alive in a body and in an actual, relational world that is right here and now. The miracle of life is not to be found in a handheld contraption, it is to be found in your own hand and the capacity you have to reach out to others. And it is to be found in your body and mind and all that surrounds you, the sea of sentient beings with whom you exchange oxygen, sunlight, starlight, food, water, love, ideas, inspiration, passion, and everything else.

Don't forget the wise words of Ram Dass: "Be Here Now." And remember that "*Here*" is a nice little planet called earth, populated with a few billion humans and a limitless supply of terrestrial beings. "*Here*" is also the community in which you live and the people with whom you share society in your town or city. It's everything and everyone with whom you come into contact. Welcome the contact. Be willing to put down your phone or handheld device, set aside digital reality, and engage the world that is alive all around you. Our reality and the planet and all that we are do not exist primarily within your cell phone. In fact, the arrangement is quite the other way around.

Bibliography

BBC. (2002). "Air Pollution Cancer Fears grow."
http://news.bbc.co.uk/2/hi/health/1853675.stm

Campbell, Joseph & Bill Moyers. *The Power of Myth*. Anchor Books, 1991.

Chief Seattle. The Speech of Chief Seattle. Applewood Books, 2000.

Clear Air Council. www.cleanair.org, 2008.

Constitution of the Iroquois Nation.
http://www.awelltendedmind.com/A_Well_Tended_Mind/Living_Within_our_Means.html

Diogenes. Bly, Robert, James Hillman, & Michael Meade (Eds.). *The Rag and Bone Shop of the Heart*. HarperPerennial, 1992.

Environmental Protection Agency. (2010). "Ozone Science: The Facts Behind the Phaseout."
http://www.epa.gov/ozone/science/sc_fact.html

Forbes, Jack. *Columbus and other Cannibals*. Seven Stories Press, 1992.

Guma, Greg. "Native Incarceration Rates Are Increasing." 2005.
http://www.towardfreedom.com/americas/140-native-incarceration-rates-are-increasing-0302

Hahn, Thich Nat. *The Miracle of Mindfulness*. Beacon Press Books, 1975.

Hesiod, *Theogony 116 ff* (trans. Evelyn-White) Greek epic C8th or C7th B.C.

Hillman, James & Michael Ventura. *We've Had a Hundred Years of Psychotherapy and the World is Getting Worse*. HarperSanFrancisco, 1992.

Lame Deer & Richard Erdoes. *Lame Deer, Seeker of Visions*. Pocket Books, 1972.

Ilene, Vicki. "Deforestation in the United States."
www.greenliving.lovetoknow.com, 2006-2012.

Jiminez, Juan Ramon. *Selected Writings of Juan Ramon Jimenez*. Edited by Eugenio Florit. Ambassador Books, 1957.

Jung, Carl. *On the Psychology of the Unconscious in Symbols of Transformation, Collected Works, Volume 5*. Princeton University Press, 1917.

—. *Memories, Dreams, Reflections*. Random House, 1961.

—. *Collected Works, Volume 13*. Princeton University Press, 1967.

—. *Two Essays on Analytical Psychology in Collected Works, Volume 7.* Princeton University Press, 1957.

Kane, Joe. *Savages.* Vintage Books, 1995.

Keen, Sam. *Faces of the Enemy.* Harper & Row, 1986

Kimerling, Judith. *Amazon Crude.* National Defenses Resource Council, 1991.

Margolin, Malcolm. *The Way We Lived: California Indian Stories, Songs & Reminiscences.* Heydey Books, 1993.

Moore, Robert & Douglas Gillette. *The Lover Within.* HarperCollins, 1993.

Morrison, Jim & Robby Krieger. *People Are Strange.* Elektra, 1967.

Neihardt, John (Ed.). *Black Elk Speaks.* William Morrow, 1932.

Paz, Octavio. *The Labyrinth of Solitude.* Grove Press, 1961.

—. *The Philanthropic Ogre.* Grove Press, 1972.

—. *Mexico and the United States.* Grove Press, 1972.

Pinchbeck, Daniel. *2012: The Return of Quetzalcoatl.* Penguin, 2007.

Plato. *Phaedrus.* Translated by R. Hackforth. Cambridge University Press, 1952.

Prechtel, Martin. *Secret of the Talking Jaguar.* Penguin Putnam, 1998.

—. *Long Life Honey in the Heart.* North Atlantic Books, 1999.

Raintree Website, 2006. http://rain-tree.com

Robbins, Tom. *Half asleep in Frog Pajamas.* Bantam Books, 1994.

Rumi, Jelaluddin. *The Essential Rumi.* Translated by Coleman Barks with John Moyne, A. J. Arberry and Reynold Nicholson. Harper San Francisco, 1995.

SABRA. "The Troubling Numbers of Job-Related Injuries." *New York Times* August 31, 1997.
http://search.nytimes.com/search/daily/bin/fastweb?getdoc+site+site+18987+0+wAAA+

Salzberg, Sharon. *Lovingkindness: The Revolutionary Art of Happiness.* Shambhala Publications, 1995.

Somé, Malidoma. *Of Water and the Spirit.* Arkana, 1994.

—. Ritual: Power, Healing, and Community. Swan/Raven & Company, 1993.

Vandenack, Tim. "Chile's Battle-ground of Culture vs. Profit." *Christian Science Monitor,* June, 2001.

Ventura, Michael. *Letters at 3am.* Spring Publications, 1993.

Waters, Roger & David Gilmore. *Wish You Were Here.* Harvest Records, 1975.

Watts, Alan. *The Joyous Cosmology.* Vintage Books, 1965.

NOTE: All statistics referenced throughout this book which are not mentioned in the Bibliography were taken from multiple online data resources and cross-checked for validity.

About the Author

Salvatore Folisi is a poet, musician, freelance writer, and the owner of Xander Stone Ink. He has published three books of poetry: *Walking The Streets in The Labyrinth of My Mind* (originally published as *Daimon: a Journey of Poems*), *For Love of a Dark Night,* and *Carnival of the Wild* as well as multiple articles in the genres of philosophy, psychology, and spirituality that have appeared in *Adbusters* Magazine, *Vision* Magazine, and various online journals. He can be reached through his website: http://xanderstone.org.